THE MAKING OF A SOUTH AFRICAN NATIONAL PARK

MARAK

PHOTOGRAPHS LOUISE AGNEW . ANDY ROUSE

PAUL VAN VLISSINGEN . TET VAN VLISSINGEN

AFRICAN PARKS

Marakele
National Park
Extension

Welgevonden
Reserve

Marakele
National Park

Special
Species
Area

W A T E R B E R G

to Thabazimbi

MARAKELE NATIONAL PARK
Schematic cadastral boundaries incorporated into Marakele
National Park and adjoining private reserves

Soestdijk Palace, June 2003

The Marakele project is an outstanding achievement by the private-public partnership between Paul van Vlissingen and South African National Parks. It shows a wonderful result and I am certain that this is probably the only way to develop protected areas in Africa.

I hope many will follow.

Prince of The Netherlands

MARAKELE NATIONAL PARK

Map of South Africa showing the location of Marakele
National Park relative to other major protected areas
and provincial boundaries

LEGEND

	Provincial Boundaries
	Study Area
o	Major Towns
	Primary Roads
	Conservation Areas
	National Parks
	Other Protected Areas
	Provincial Boundaries
	Eastern Cape
	Free State
	Gauteng
	Kwazulu-Natal
	Lesotho
	Mpumalanga
	North-West
	Northern Cape
	Northern Province
	Swaziland
	Western Cape

South African
NATIONAL PARKS

0   100   200 kilometres

Scale 1:5500000

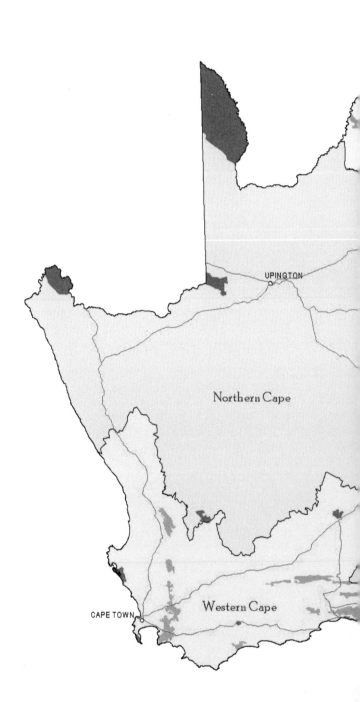

UPINGTON

Northern Cape

CAPE TOWN

Western Cape

This book is dedicated to Mavuso Msimang,
above all a friend.

First published in 2003 by African Parks B.V.
Langbroekerdijk A97, 3947 BE Langbroek, The Netherlands

Available in North, South and Central America, and Asia through D.A.P./
Distributed Art Publishers Inc, 155 Sixth Avenue 2nd Floor, New York,
NY 10013-1507, USA, Tel +1 212 6271999, Fax +1 212 6279484
dap@dapinc.com

Available in the United Kingdom and Ireland through Art Data,
12 Bell Industrial Estate, 50 Cunnington Street, London W4 5HB, UK,
Tel +44 20 87471061, Fax +44 20 87422319
orders@artdata.co.uk

Available in Europe through Coen Sligting Bookimport,
Van Oldenbarneveldtstraat 77, 1052 JW Amsterdam, The Netherlands,
Tel +31 20 6732280, Fax +31 20 6640047
sligting@xs4all.nl

Photographs: Louise Agnew, Andy Rouse, Paul van Vlissingen, Tet van Vlissingen
Text: Paul Fentener van Vlissingen
Poem and film 'Marakele, the making of a National Park': Caroline Tisdall
Design & image editing: irmaboom@xs4all.nl

Printed and bound in The Netherlands

ISBN 90-808037-1-5

CONTENTS

THE MARAKELE STORY

This is a story about nature, animals, and people. It is a story about personal commitment and collective dedication, about putting existing natural resources to the best use and about public–private partnership. It is about an innovative approach developed in Marakele National Park which could become a model for saving the irreplaceable gems of sub-Saharan Africa: its national parks.

IN THE BEGINNING

A few years ago, I had the privilege to be introduced to President Nelson Mandela. I asked him about his government's policy on the protection and expansion of Africa's wild places – its national parks. President Mandela replied that there was little money for parks, as there were many more pressing needs, such as the provision of educational facilities, housing, water, sewerage systems, hospitals, a better police force – 'Our voters will not understand if we put a lot of money into zebras while they live without a roof over their heads.' Mandela opened my eyes.

The story had a second father: Mavuso Msimang, the invaluable and able Zulu CEO of South African National Parks. Realistic, seasoned by experience and well equipped to handle the crises and intrigues of post-apartheid national parks (he was trained in Moscow in urban warfare), he saw the need for a new approach to park management and understood how this could involve the private sector.

Valli Moosa, the government minister responsible for the environment, strongly supported this new concept of public–private partnership for national parks.

THE MARAKELE MODEL

Marakele National Park has one of the most accessible and breathtaking land-scapes in South Africa. Only a few hours' drive north of Johannesburg, it musters a diverse combination of fantastic mountains and gorges, bush and plains, rivers and ponds. But when I found it in 1997, it was stagnating. There was no money, no hope of achieving the expansion of lowland areas that was needed for the animals' feeding range, or of building and maintaining fences.

There were dedicated individuals to do the work, but there was no money to maintain and reinvigorate the park or to invest in a strategy of biodiversity. Access was difficult, game species and population levels were declining. Facilities such as tent camps were lacking; and there were practically no visitors.

Simply providing money would not have been a sustainable solution. There had to be a broader strategy based on a model of public–private partnership, where both parties could focus on what they do best. The state would provide the land and legislative framework. The private sector would provide funds after careful economic analysis, under strict budgetary contraints, and within a clear accounting framework. It would also provide management expertise to allow for a culture of swift decision-making and to reintroduce the sense of purpose and strategy so necessary for success.

Based on a 30-year business contract, South African National Parks agreed to delegate the management and development of the northern area of Marakele to a joint management team. The management of the rest of the park would benefit from an agreement of mutual support.

It certainly was a challenge, a joint venture between two cultures, between the state and the private sector. Though it was unusual and innovative, we proved that such a partnership could yield results that were superior to a purely public approach.

The scheme was set up and implemented with splendid support from people within the government department responsible , South African National Parks, who appreciated the importance of making Marakele National Park a successful model for nature conservation.

We brought together a dedicated group of South Africans to activate the project. Within a period of two years we purchased over a dozen farms, negotiated fence removal with neighbours, relocated tent camps, developed caravan, barbecue and day-visit facilities, built and operated new entrances, constructed over 150 km of new game fencing, removed 7,000 km of barbed wire, 80 km of high-voltage power lines, 100 km of telephone cables, cleared 5,000 hectares of bush, and built a small village for the local community, whose members now own land and houses in their own name. Schools were adopted, their roofs repaired, toilets rebuilt, and uniforms, books and teaching aids supplied, as were bicycles for those pupils living a long way away. Beds were provided for a hostel, and a scholarship was set up for the best pupil to continue to higher education. The entire programme was completed within the planned span of two years.

Tourist activities will now be the financial pump to maintain and expand the park. New partners who subscribe to the principle of ecological management are welcome to participate. Large areas are available for inclusion. Farmers who decide to bring in their land will retain ownership and will be granted the right to develop eco-tourism and thus benefit from all the advantages of the unified Marakele habitat and the Park's services. However, they must agree to concede to the Park the right of first refusal in the event that they want to sell their property outside their family. Tourism and associated services will provide a range of new jobs and oppor-tunities for the local population.

National parks can only prosper if local people benefit from the management of the park. This means primarily employment as rangers and in many jobs in the tourist camps. A 50-bed camp facility for overseas visitors can provide over 100 permanent jobs. Local arts can be sold and organic gardens developed. Small businesses will benefit from increased economic input in the area.

THE NEED FOR A NEW APPROACH

All African governments face a similar dilemma: in a desperate situation of overwhelming human needs and limited funds, wildlife slips inevitably from low to last on the priority list. In addition, the vast wildlife resources of sub-Saharan Africa have not been managed to help address precisely these pressing human needs, such as food and employment.

Marakele is not a one-off case. Throughout sub-Saharan Africa, national parks were established during colonial times and were often regarded as a 'white man's hobby'. Since then, a generation of well-trained park wardens has retired and been replaced by – mostly politically appointed – people with little motivation or managerial experience. The dull hand of bureaucracy has stifled new ideas and initiatives; sources of finance have dried up; and in many countries the culture of getting things done has declined into inertia and indifference.

Overall, this has produced mediocre or bad management, which in some instances has encouraged survival by corruption and deceit. This is all part of a larger picture that includes devastation wrought by civil war, hunger, crime, and HIV/AIDS. Some national parks only exist on paper as an area on a map surrounded by a green line. Many have had their game decimated, shot or starved during civil war. Many have been invaded by people simply trying to stay alive.

The model of private-public partnership works: the state contributes land and provides the legislative framework; the private sector supplies initial funds, management, and sustainable commitment. Together, they can develop tourism activities to make the park economiccaly self-sufficient. Marakele aims to be just that from 2004 on.

The vision of Nelson Mandela, the support of Minister Valli Moosa, and the commitment and courage of Mavuso Msimang to step into the unknown have created a success, an effective new strategy for national parks. It was a privilege and pleasure to head the team that put this into effect and to see its endeavours rewarded: it works!

With its spectacular scenery and great diversity of flora and fauna, Marakele now rivals the Kruger National Park. The neighbouring private game reserve joined forces, and after taking down all fences the greater Marakele area is now approximately 120,000 hectares.

GOING FORWARD

Let us look beyond the borders of South Africa to other countries. There is every reason to develop the Marakele model of cooperation in Malawi, Mozambique, Uganda and Zambia – in fact, in all the countries of our planet where biodiversity and oases of nature are struggling to survive against the ever-increasing pressure of humankind. In generations to come, population control must be the foremost human contribution to the survival of the planet's ecosystems, as the quest for living space and agricultural land will continue to take its toll on nature and to deplete precious resources. However, time is running out. We need to develop models for the short and medium term to preserve the sub-Saharan wildlife and to manage it as a resource for sustainable development.

The position of national parks within the bureaucratic structure of government reduces the prospect of adequate financing and effective management. They are beset by external pressures – farming, tourism, building development and poaching, to which they have no adequate response. National parks cannot survive through land ownership and legislation alone: they must develop dynamic and cooperative management systems that equip them to survive in our times – and beyond.

The private–public partnership, which has been so successful at Marakele, points a way forward. It also allows for extending parks through contract management with neighbours, and thus avoids increasingly heavy land acquisition costs. Under management contract, private landowners can develop their own business while their land extends the ecologically protected area. This approach consists of developing self-financing and sustainable management systems. This is particularly the case where protected areas form the centre of a wider landscape and socio-economic systems based on the use of natural resources.

Marakele was just the beginning. What started with an inspiring conversation with Nelson Mandela has become a systematic and strategic approach that addresses the pressing needs of people living in or around national parks as well as of the animals and nature. It requires a change from managing land to managing biodiversity over much larger areas. Ecological expertise is available. Private partners will supply the practical management.

The exciting Marakele model has enormous potential for bringing about significant change to benefit people, animals and nature in the wider area of sub-Saharan Africa. To develop and expand this, funds are needed from Europe, Japan and the USA to invest in surrounding infrastructure and to finance some of the groundwork in the parks to allow for their sustainable development.

I am convinced that there is the political will in these countries to support a strategy that has proved to be viable, effective, accountable, and transparent and which is managed in a modern way. It provides an alternative to existing development schemes, as it integrates the interests of humans and nature in a sustainable manner and provides a remedy to the short- and medium-term threats to the world's most precious ecosystems and wildlife sanctuaries.

There is work to be done.

PAUL VAN VLISSINGEN
Marakele, 28 August 2003

For further information about African Parks
please contact: info@africanparks-conservation.com

POEM FOR MANDELA

I am the land.
I am Africa.
I rose with the mists of time.
Over my great cliffs and rocks
the seasons flowed like water
generous and fierce.
Nature provided
and nature was respected
in all her bounty and wildness.

But there came people
who did not respect nature.
Traders and big game hunters came first.
They stripped my plains for trophies and ivory.
And settlers changed the face
of the land beyond recognition.
Now land was bought and sold.
Now people were pushed off the land
or wiped out.
Now the animals who roamed the plains
lost their habitat.

Roads came in.
Railways came in.
Fences went up
and cattle came in.

I am the land.
I am so old, and so young.
Mankind is here for a fleeting moment,
yet has the power to destroy
or save the earth.
Hope stirs in my ancient hills:
let's plan for 6 generations ahead!

CAROLINE TISDALL

TO STAND

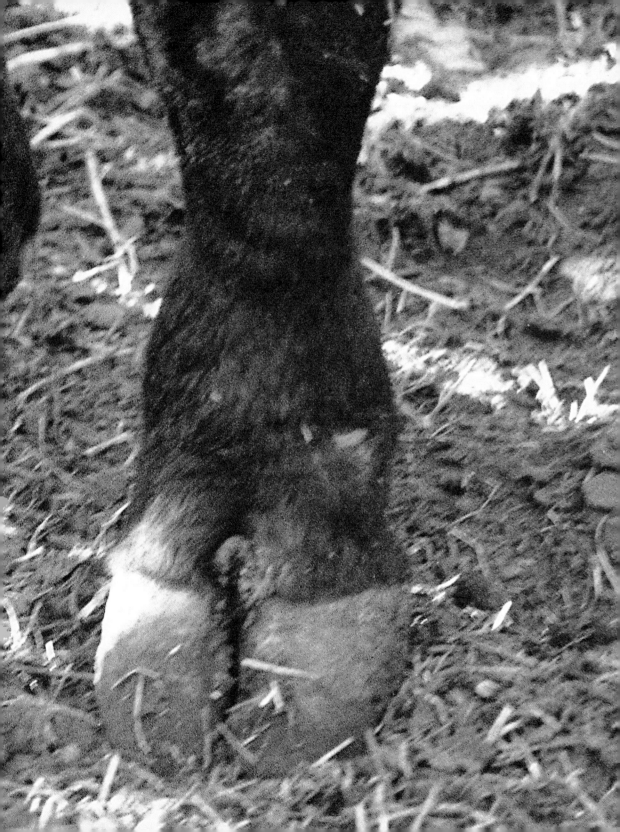

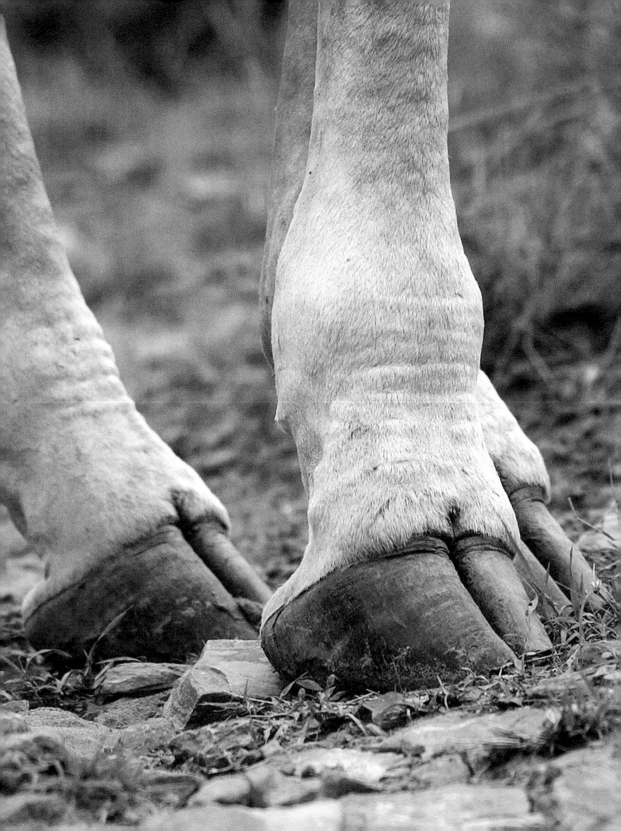

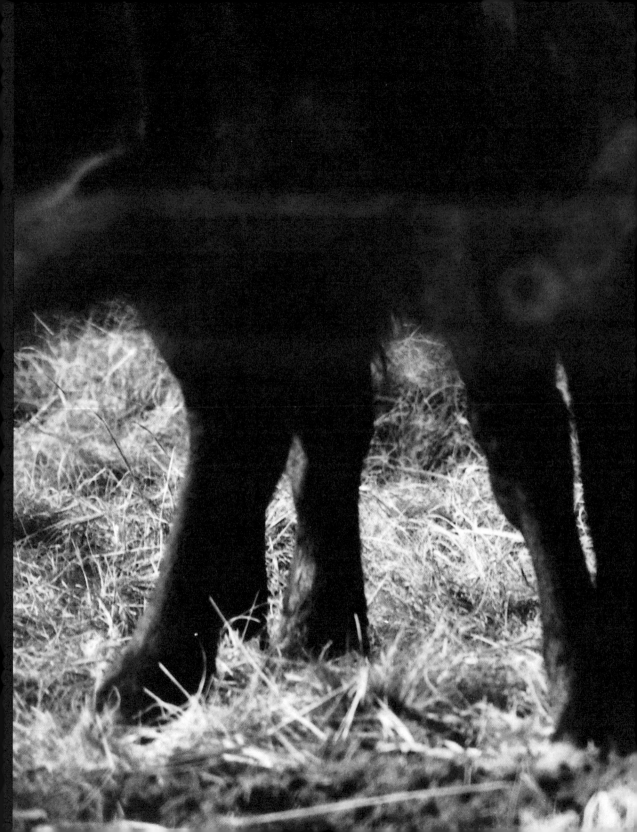

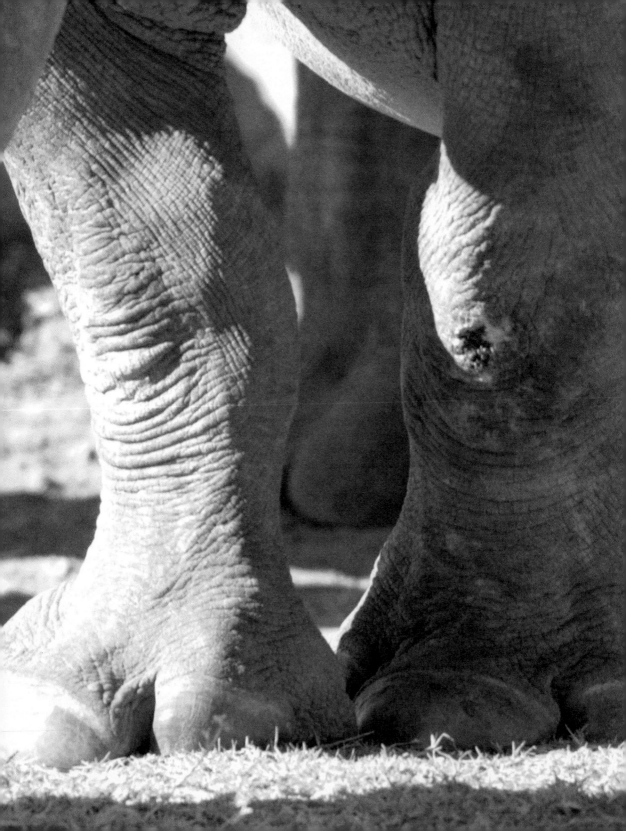

TO WAG

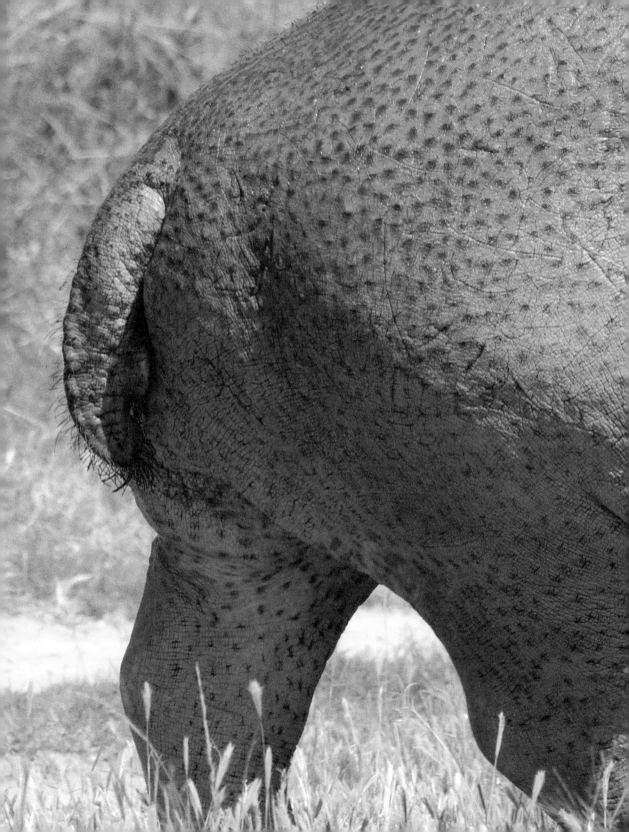

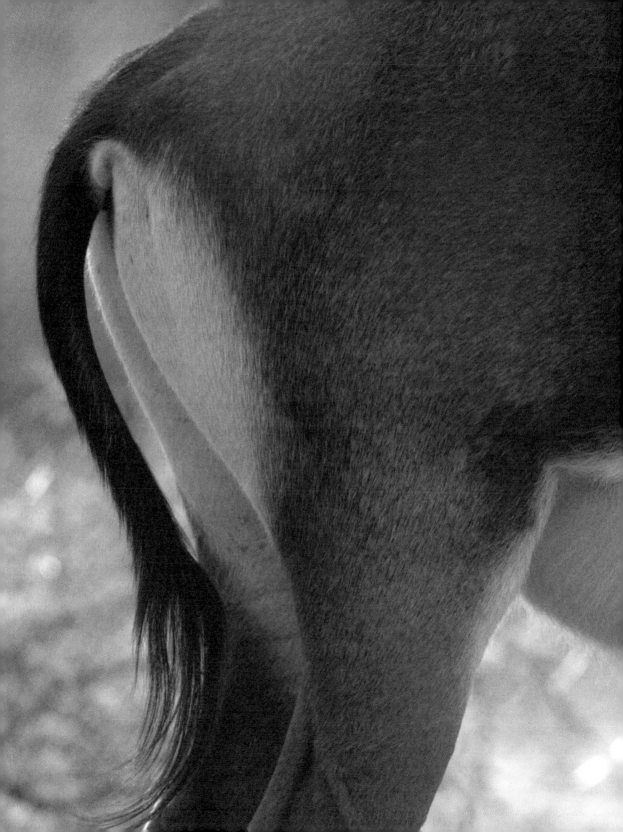

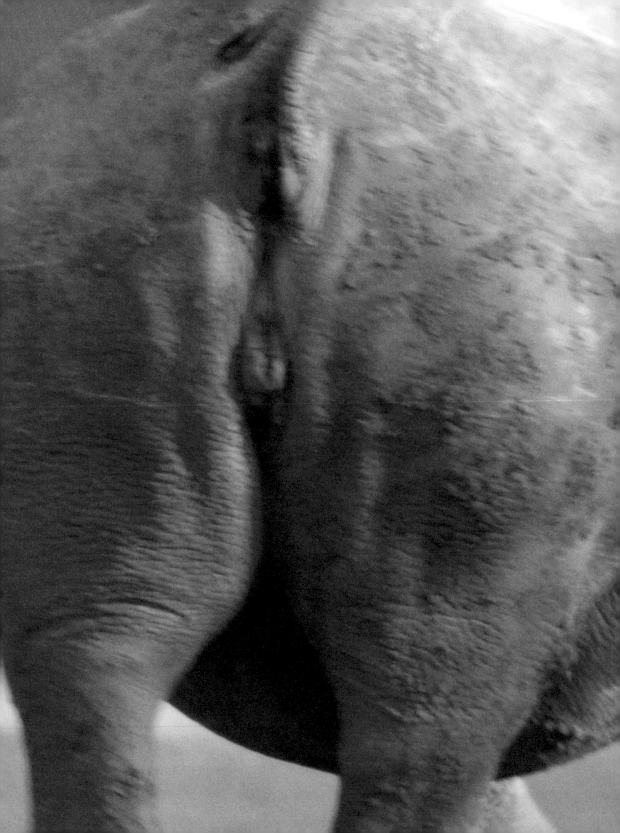

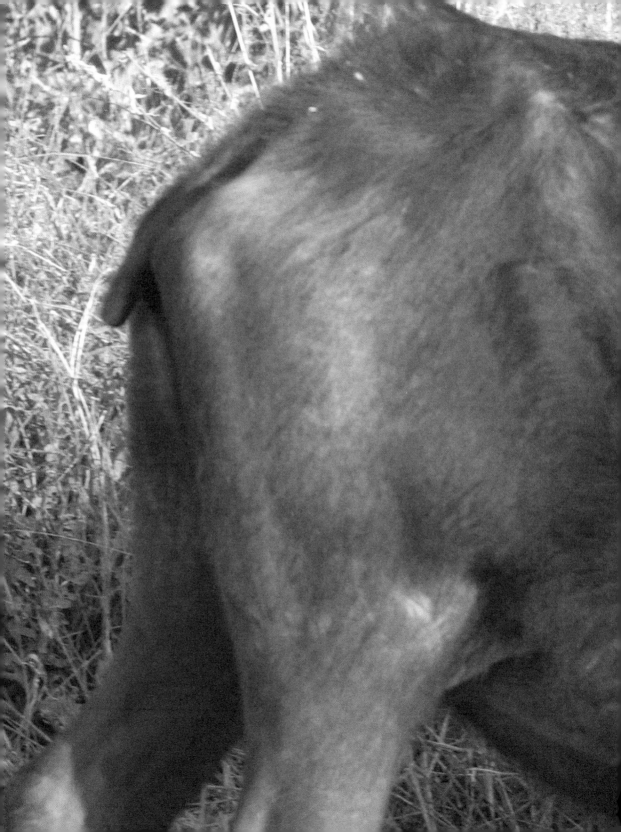

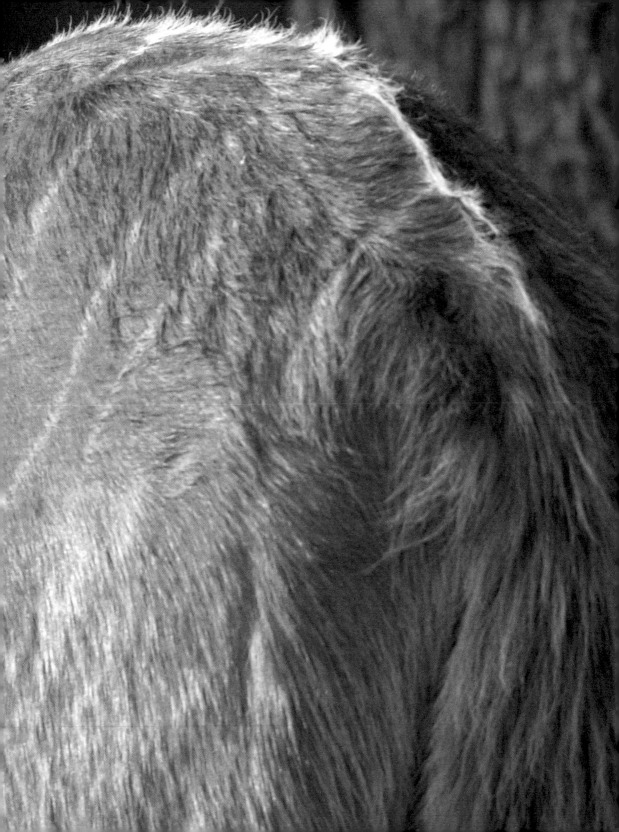

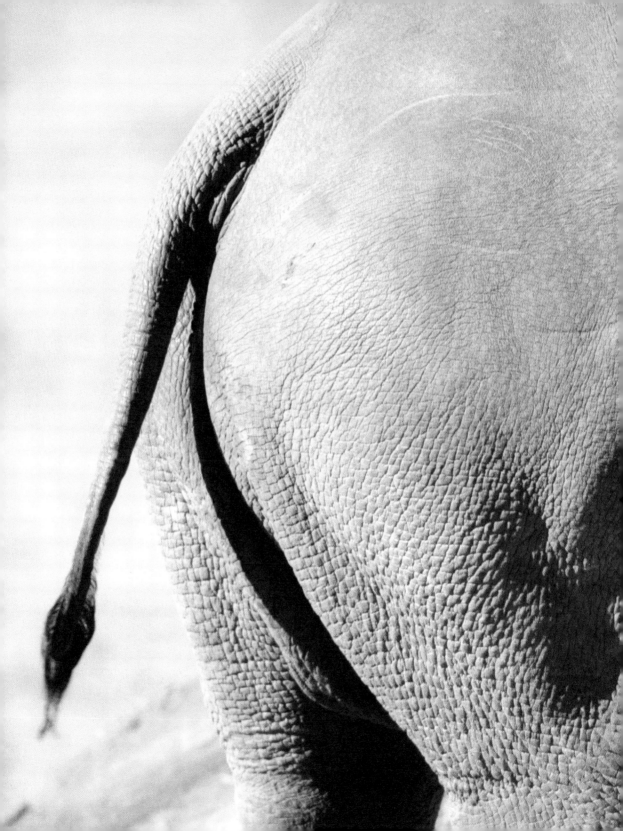

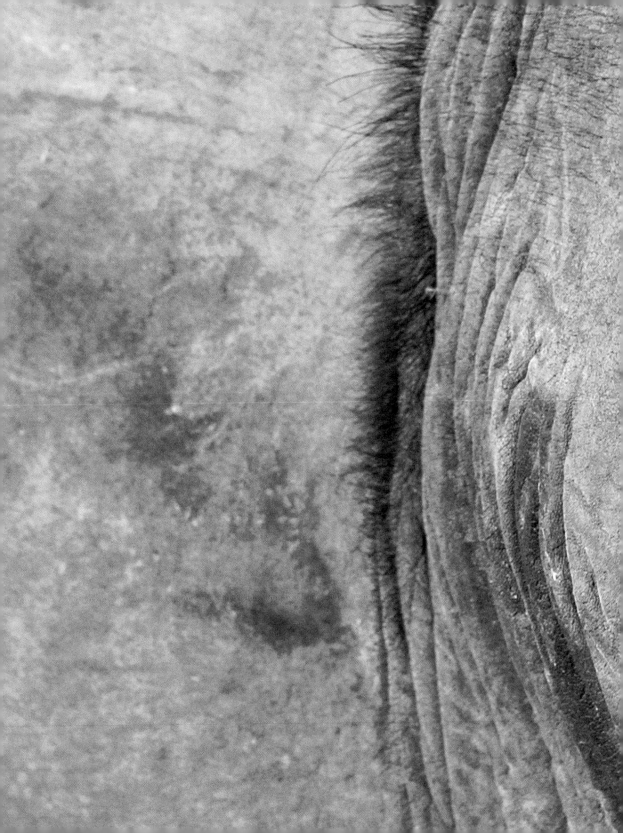

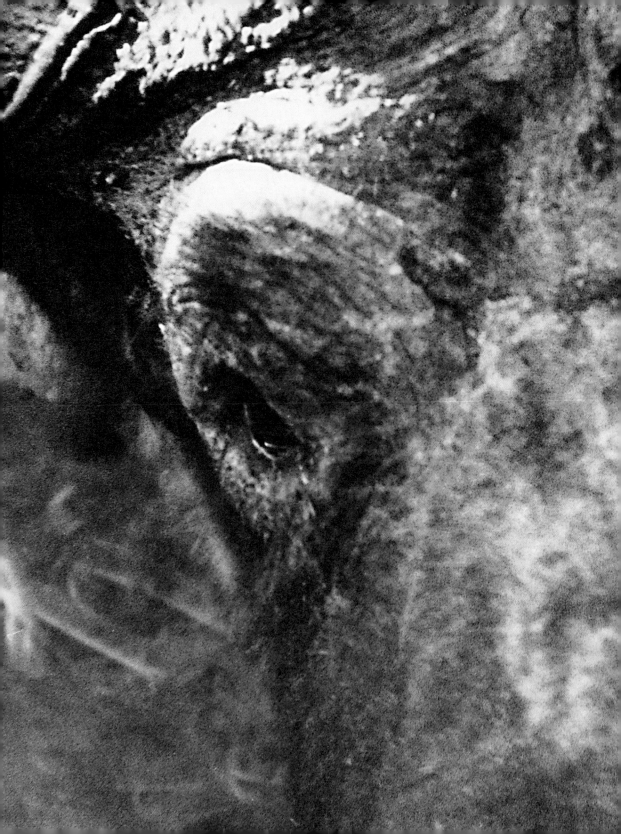

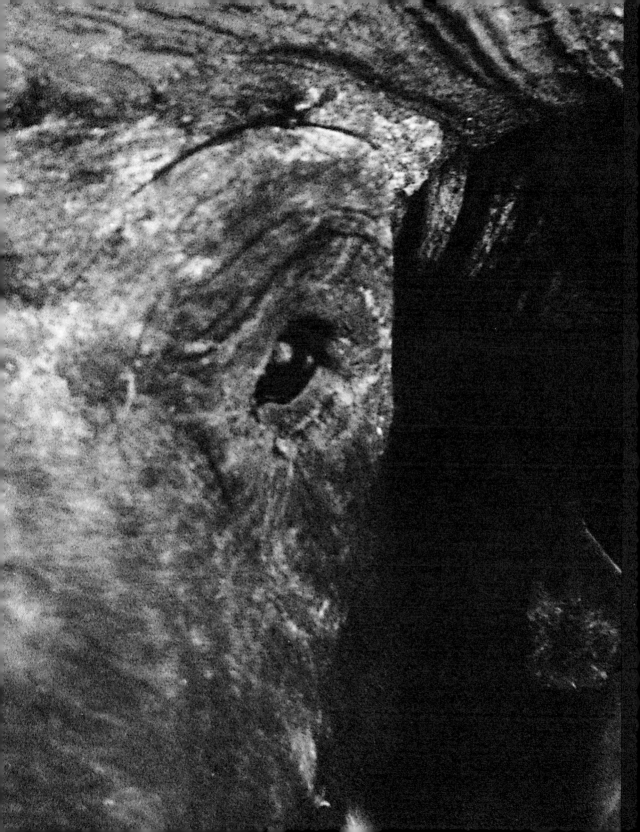

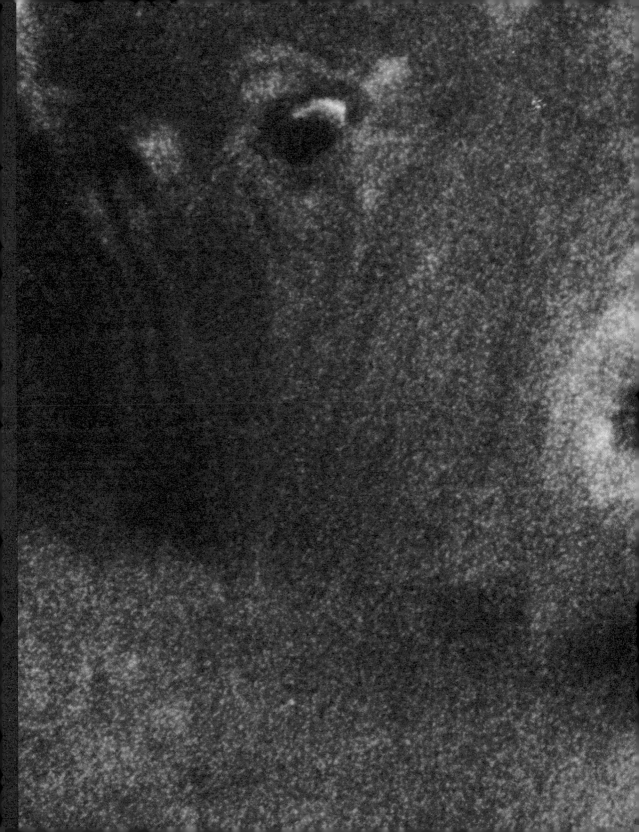

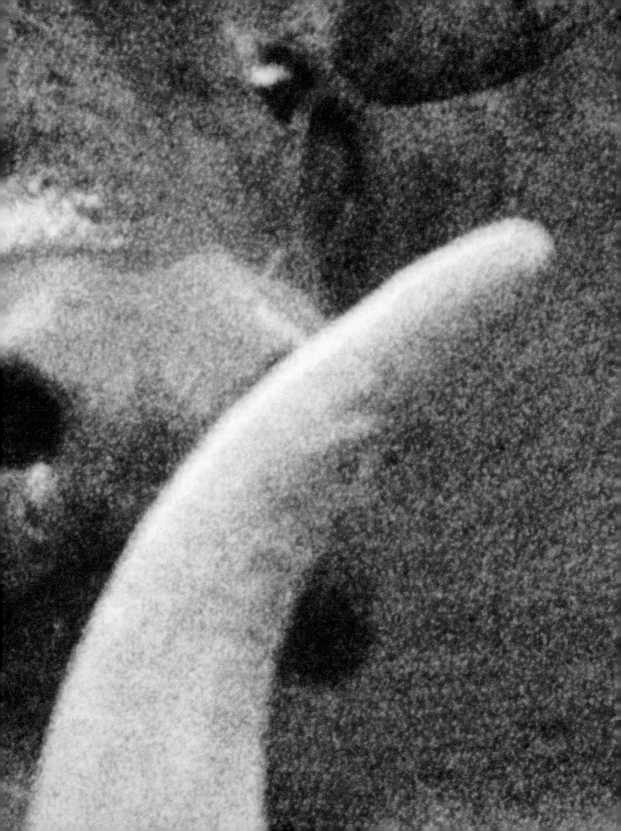

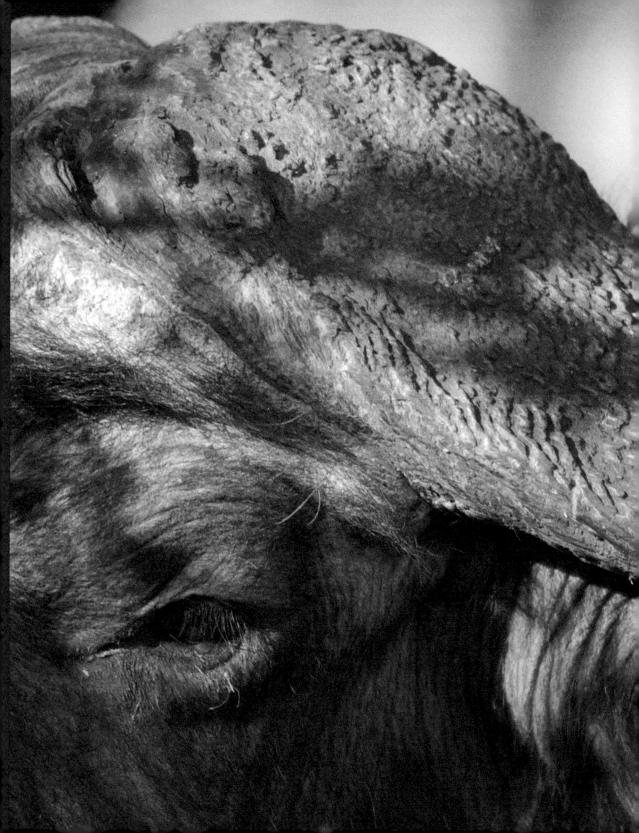

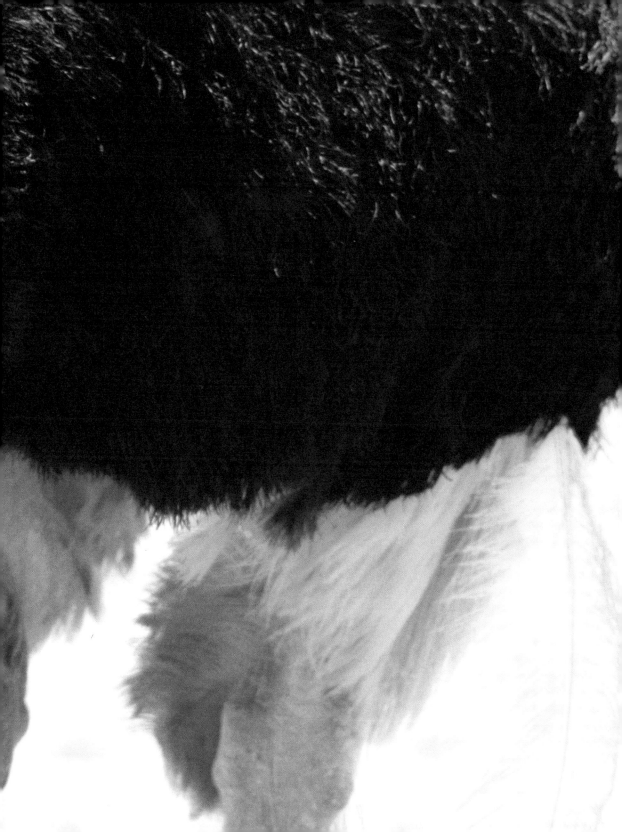

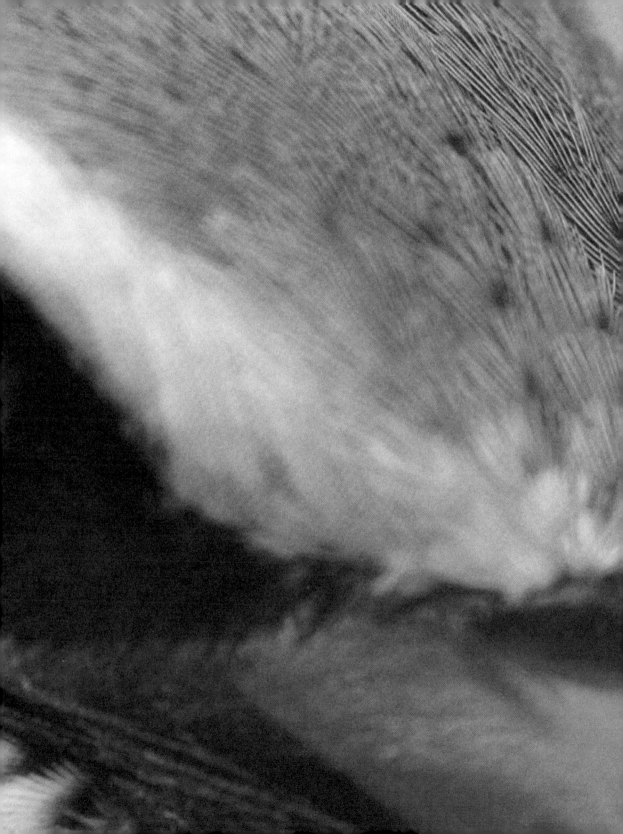

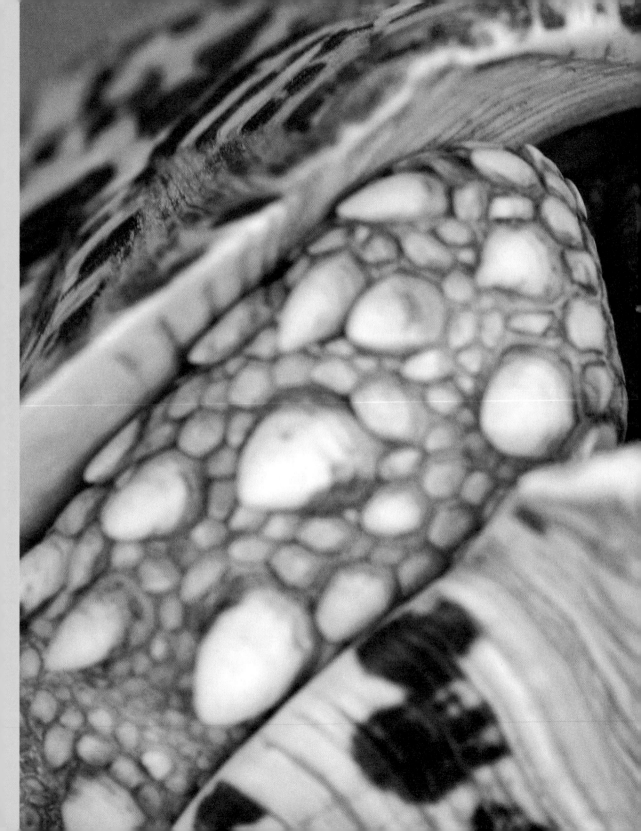

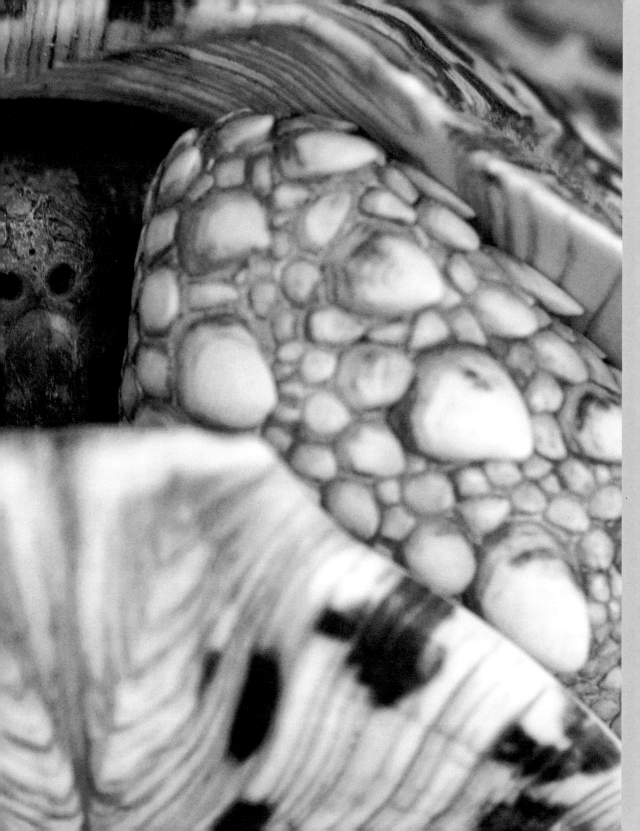

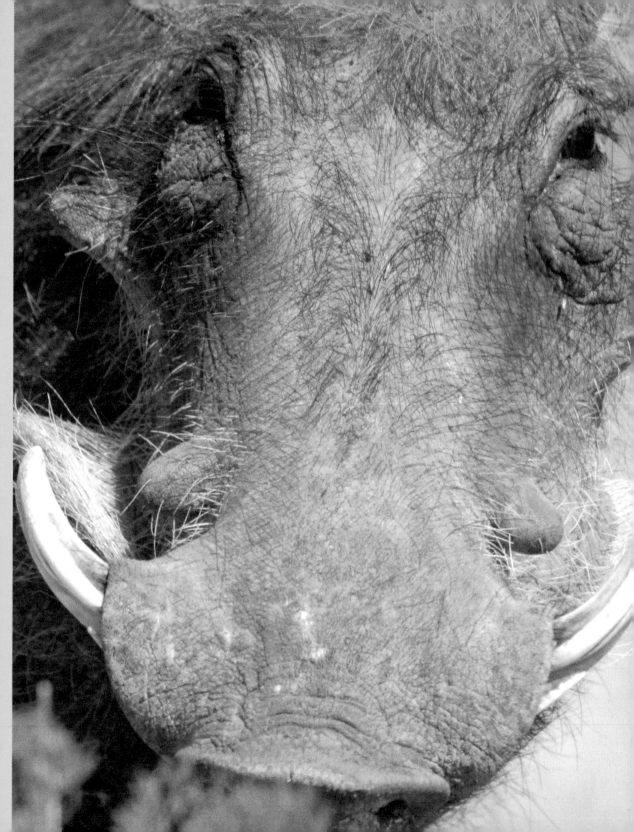

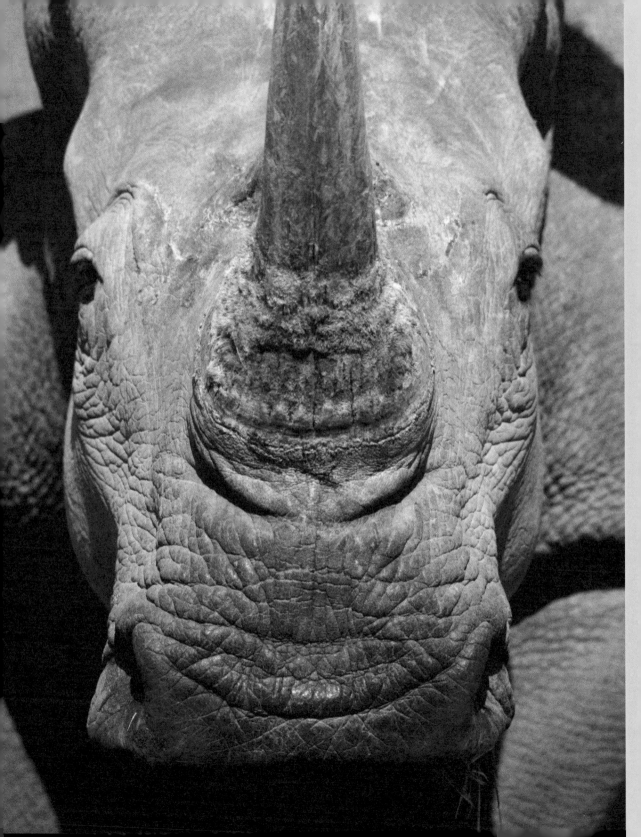

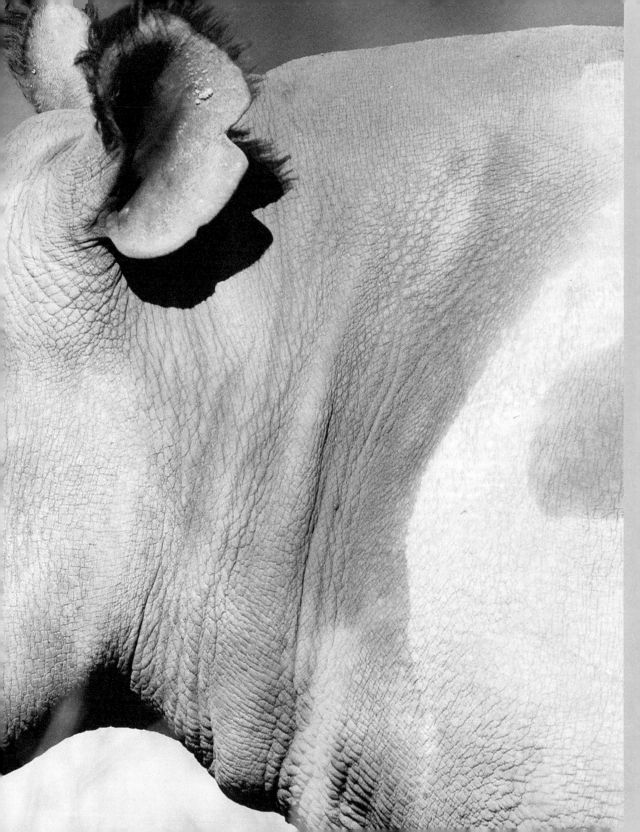

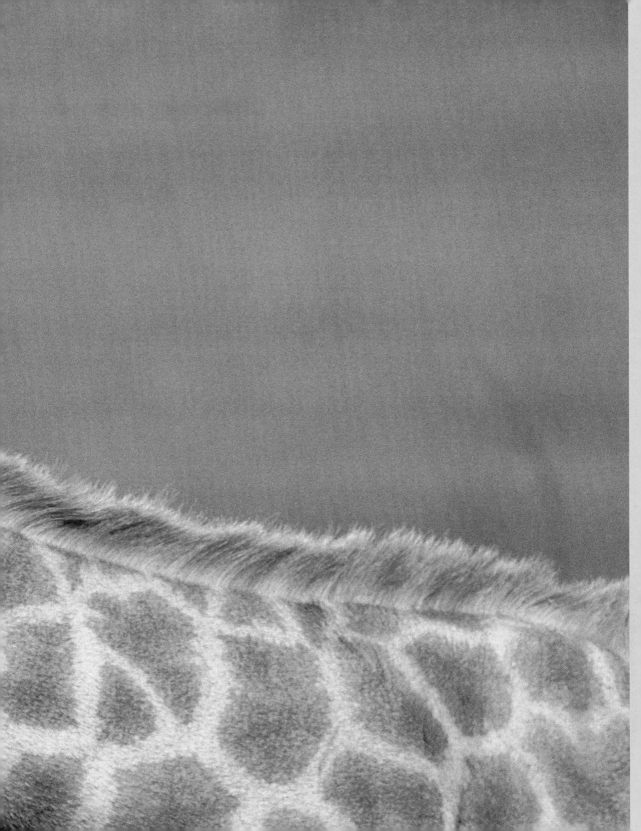

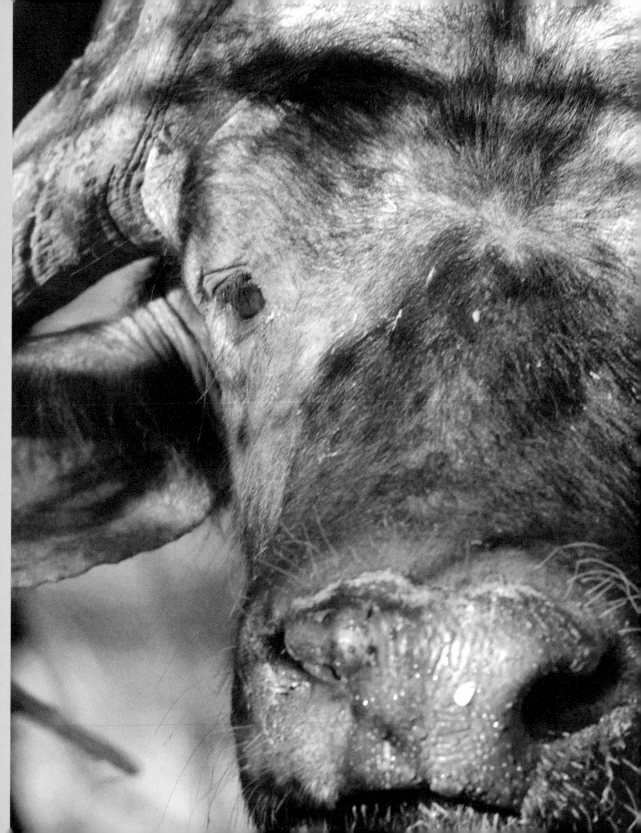

TO BREED

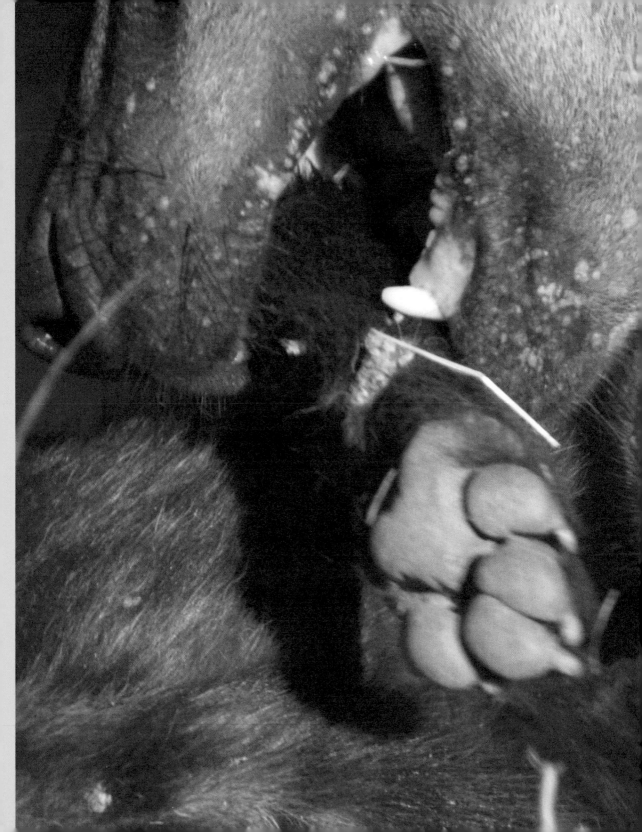

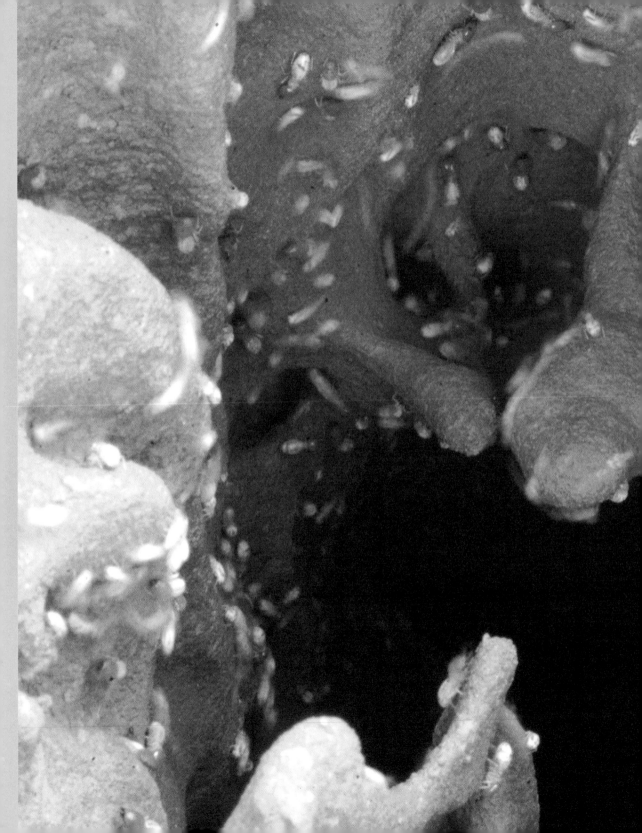

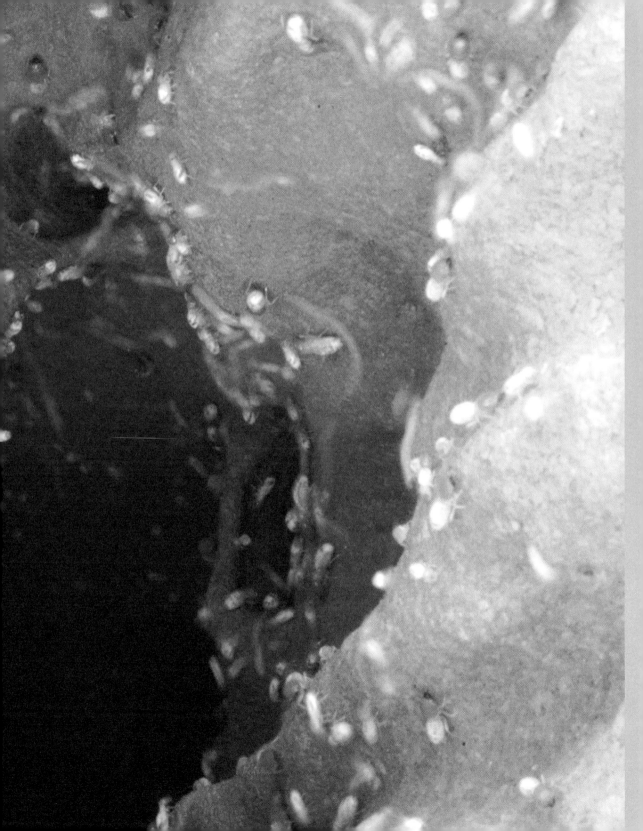

TO FLEE

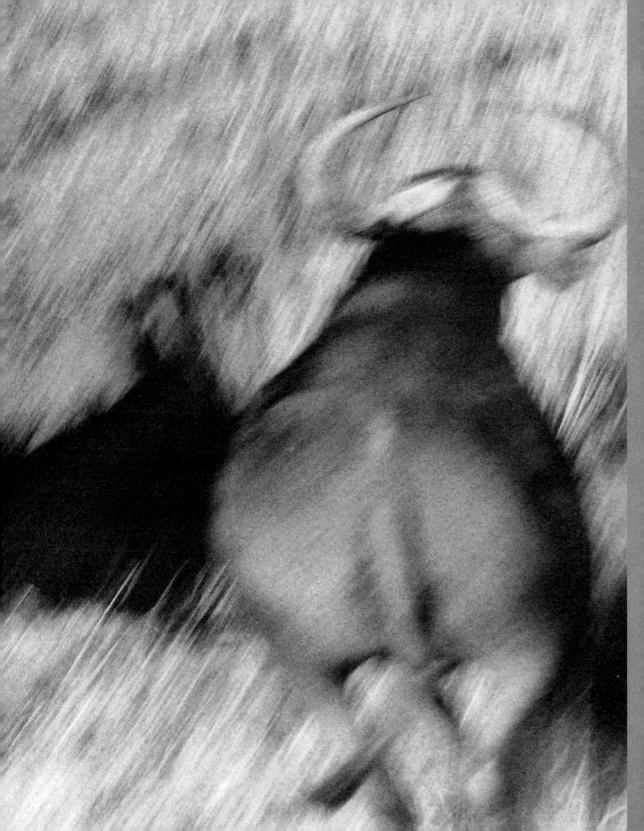

TO ASSEMBLE

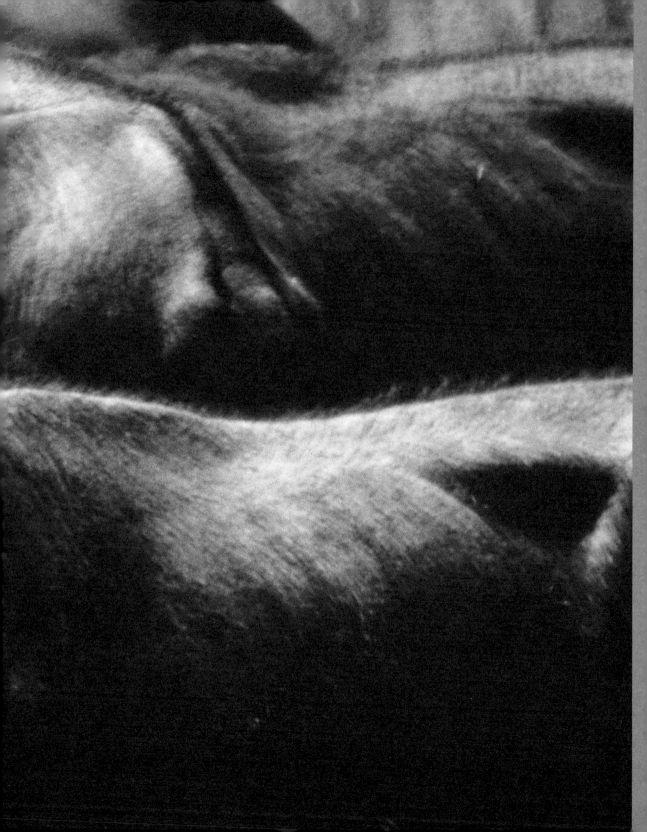

TO EAT

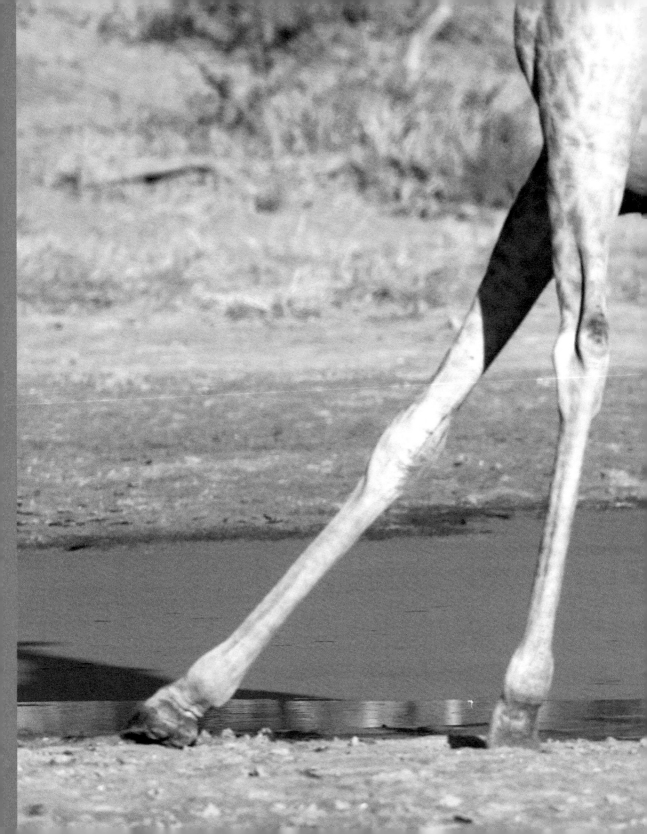

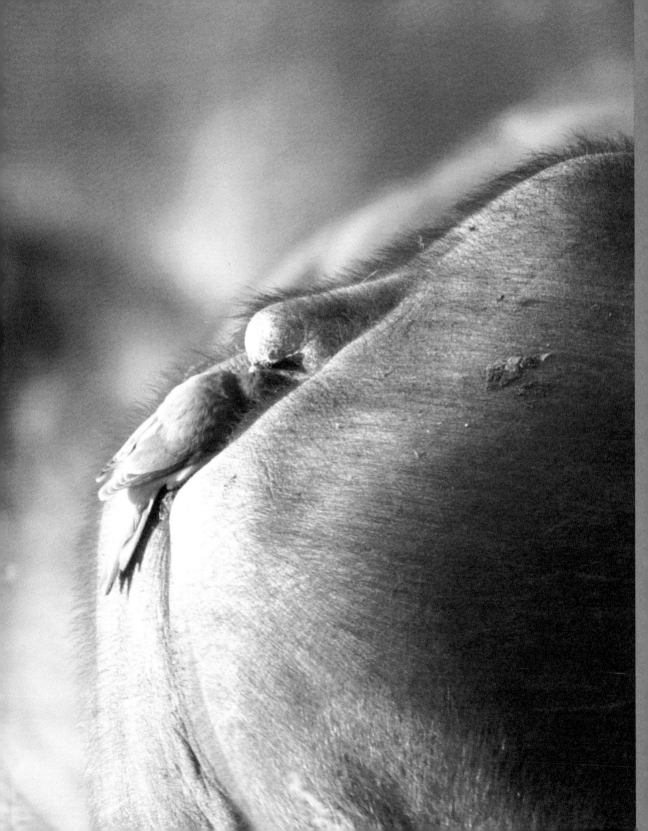

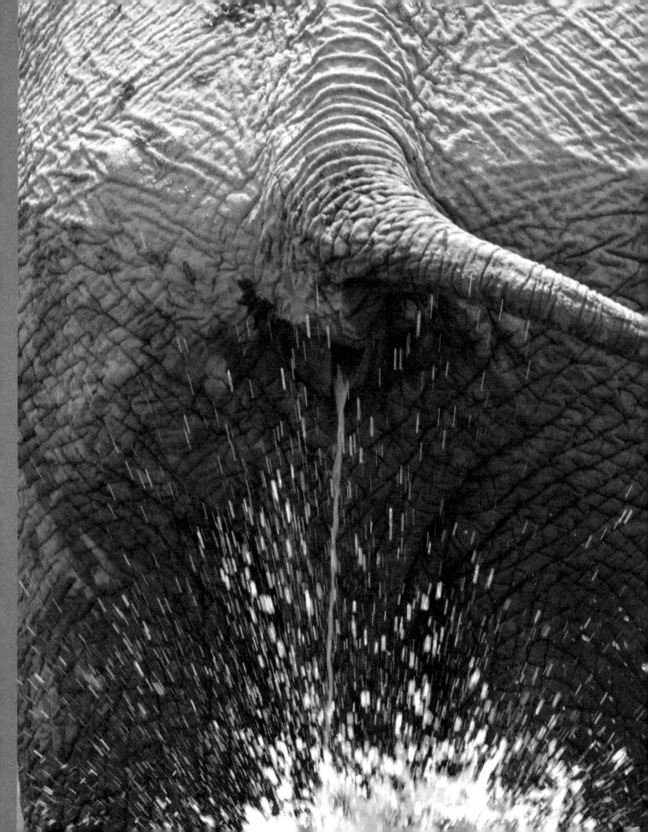

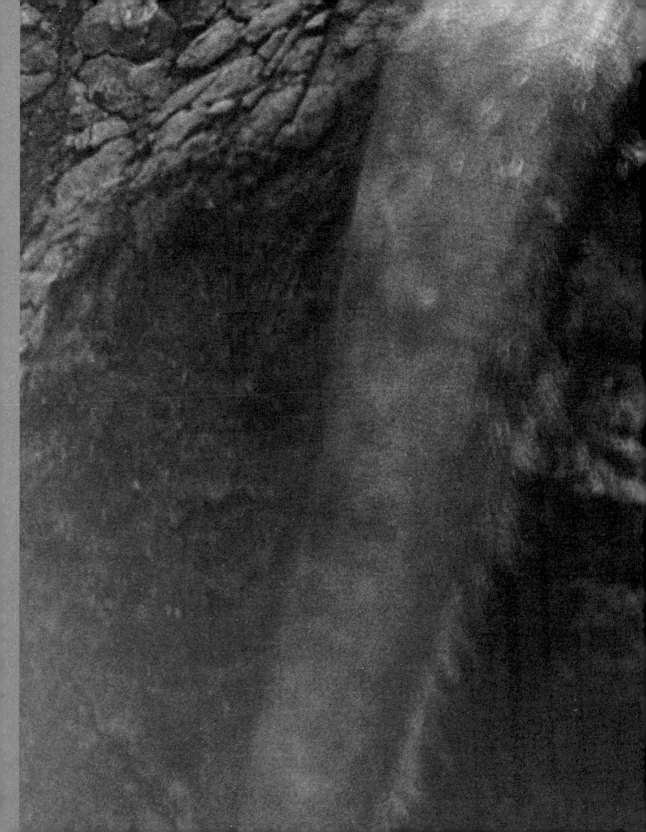

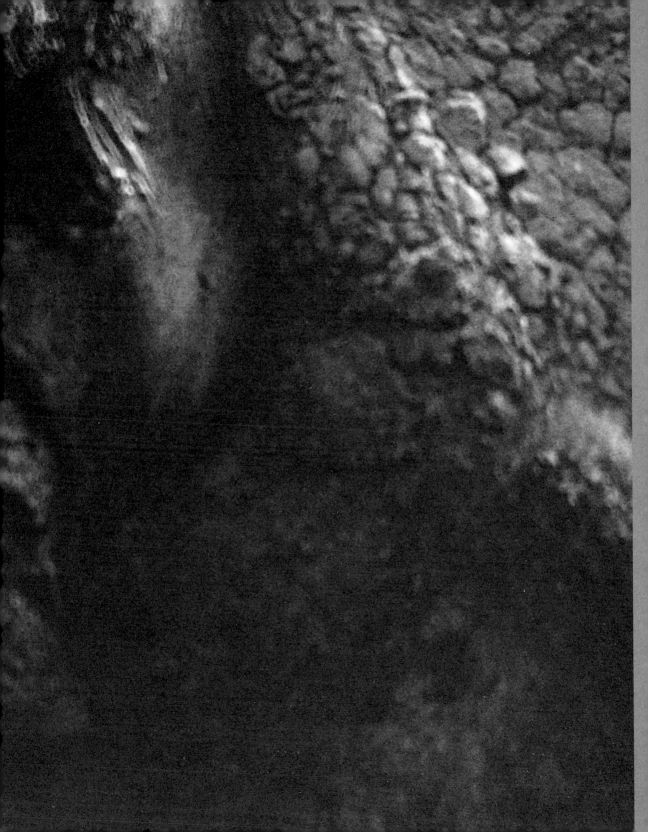

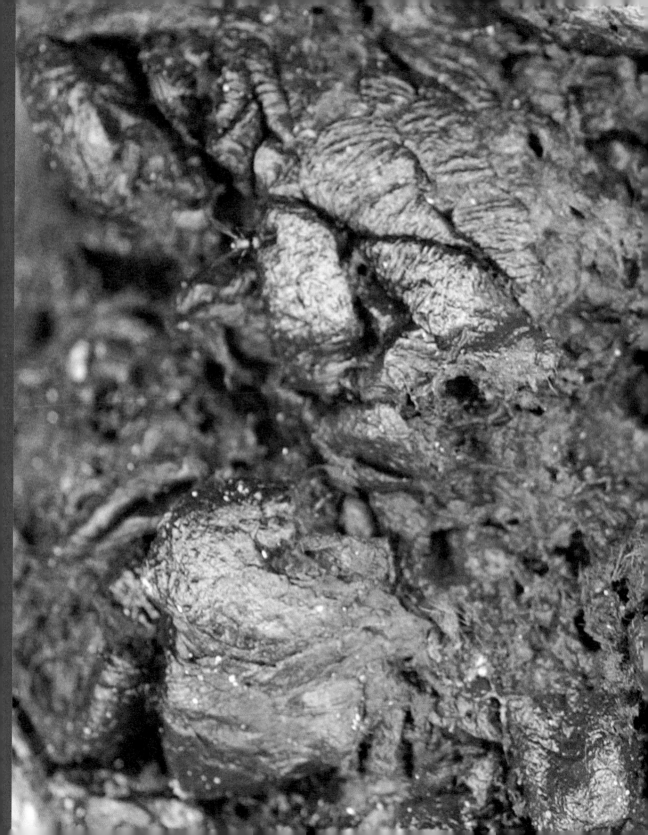

TO HIDE

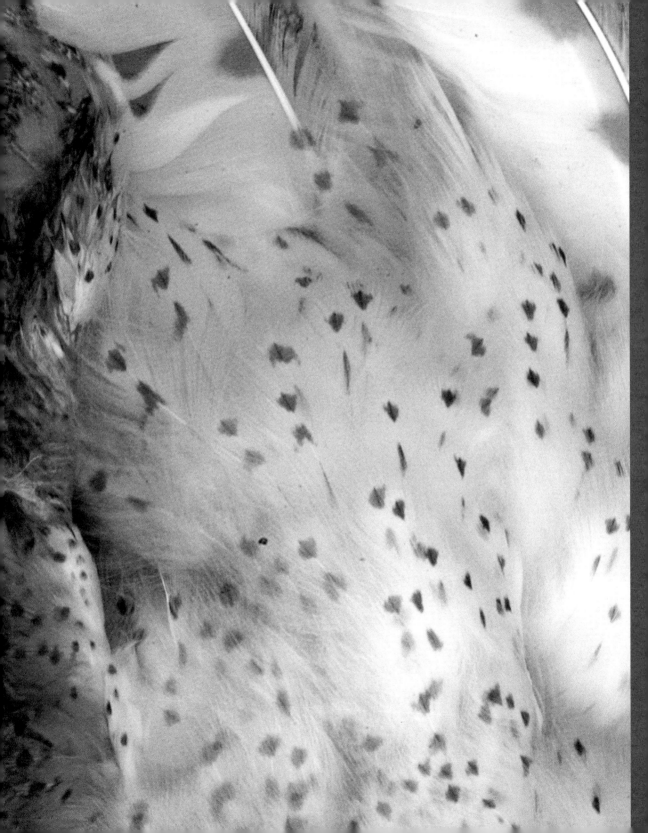

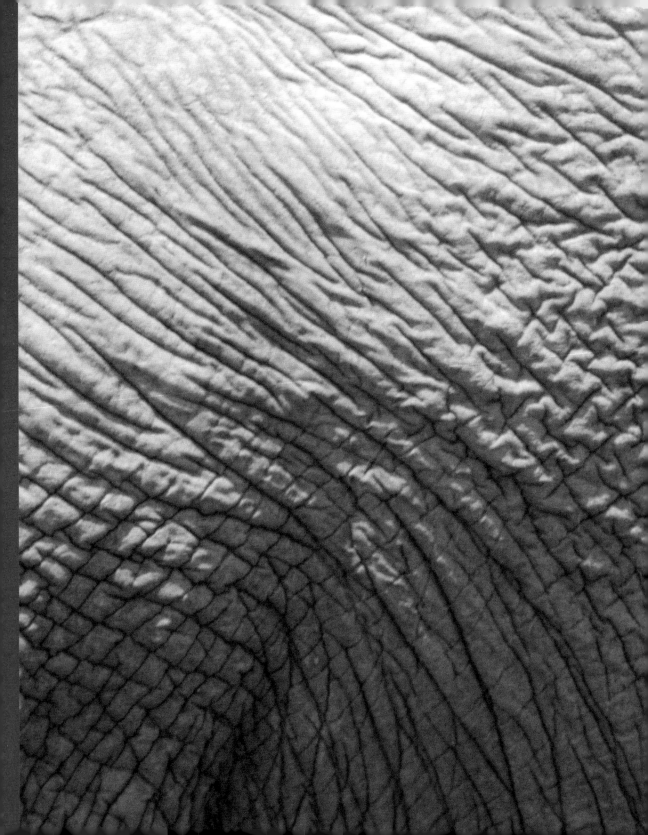

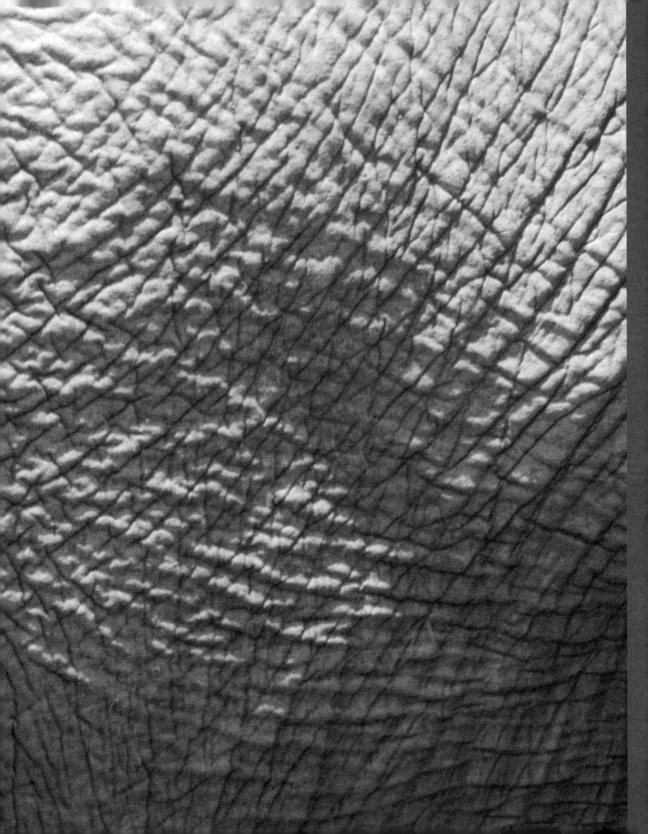

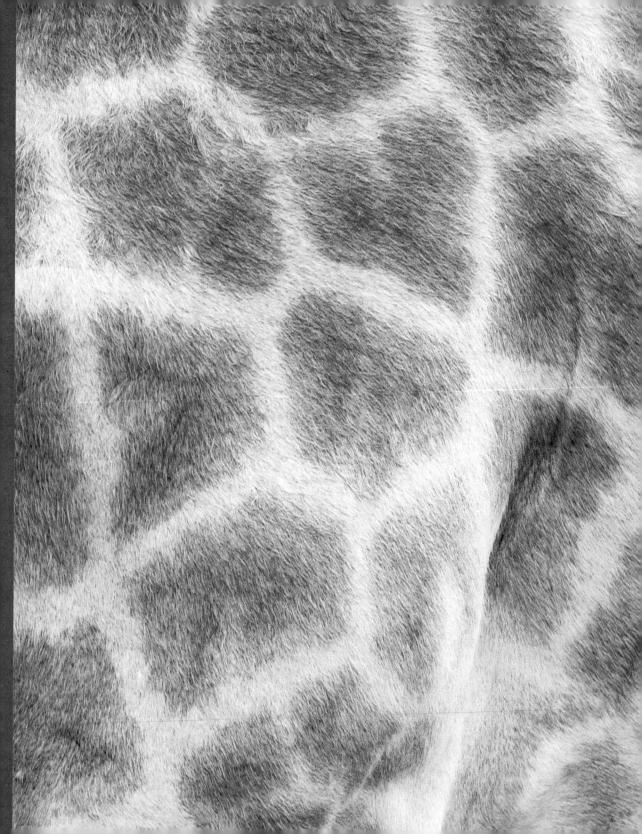

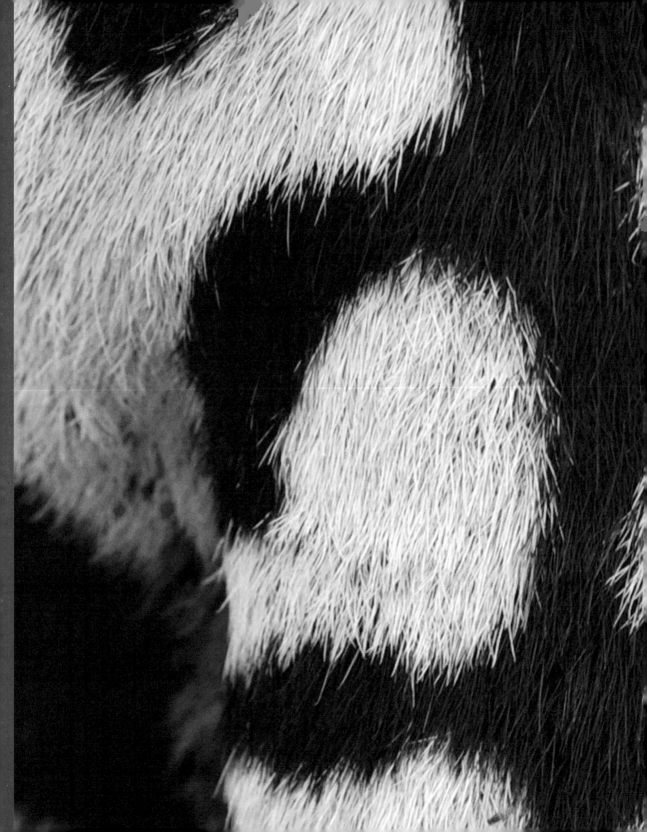

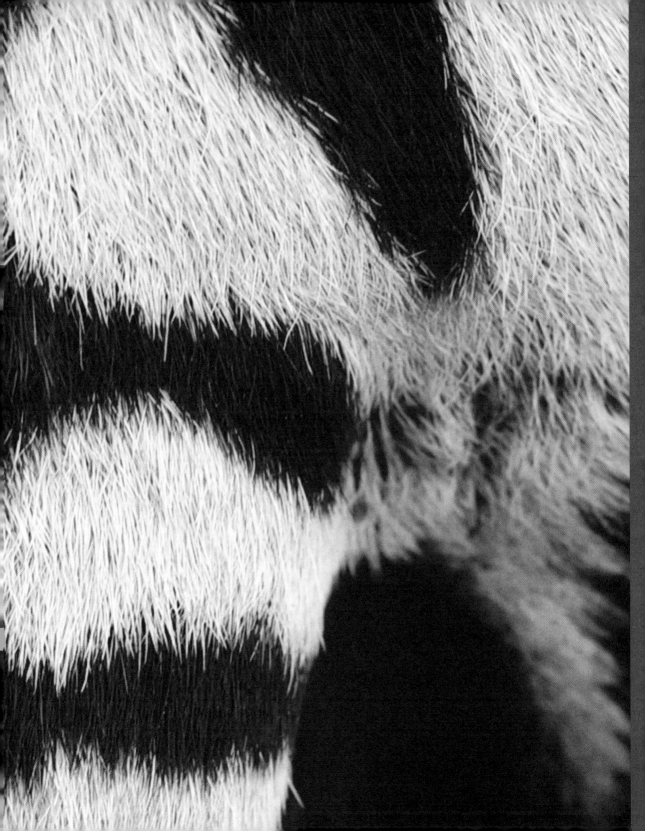

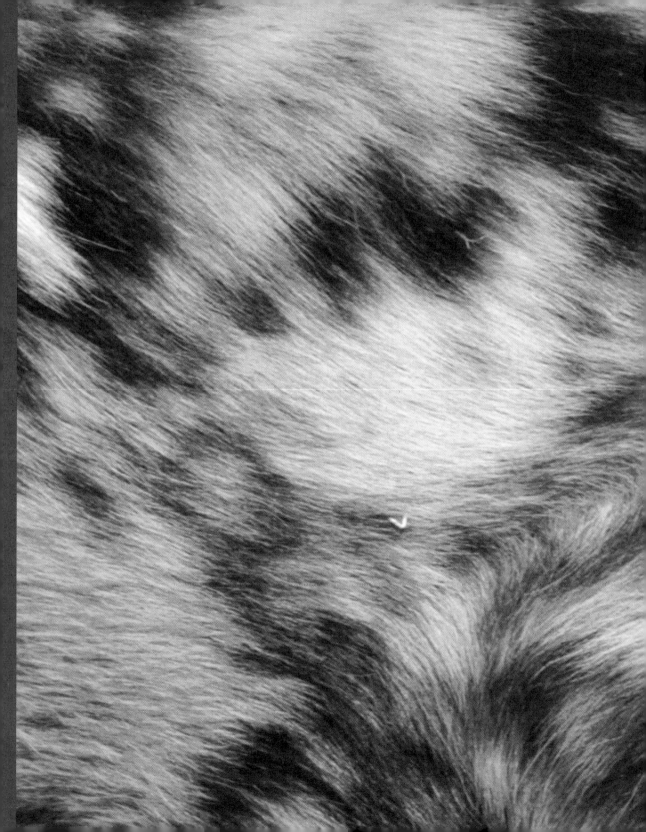

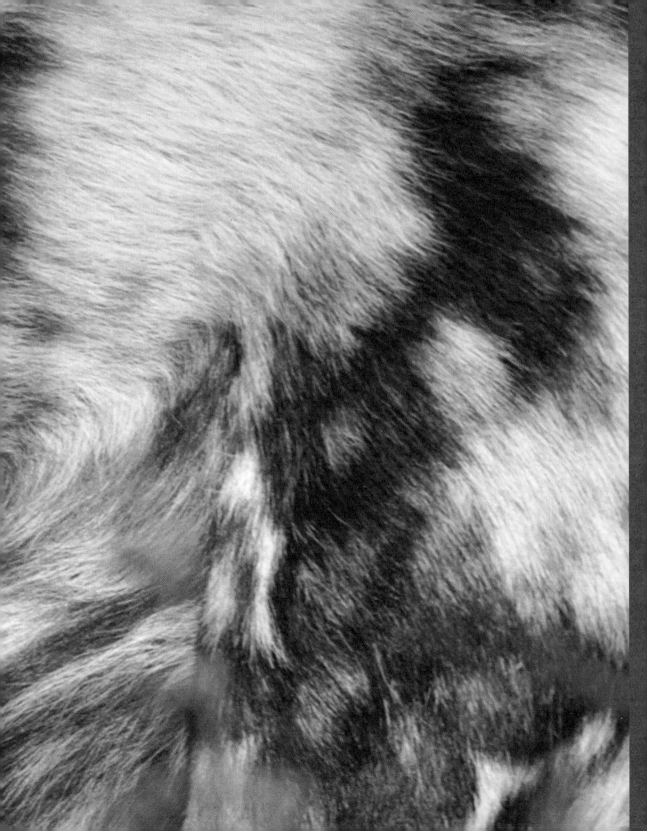

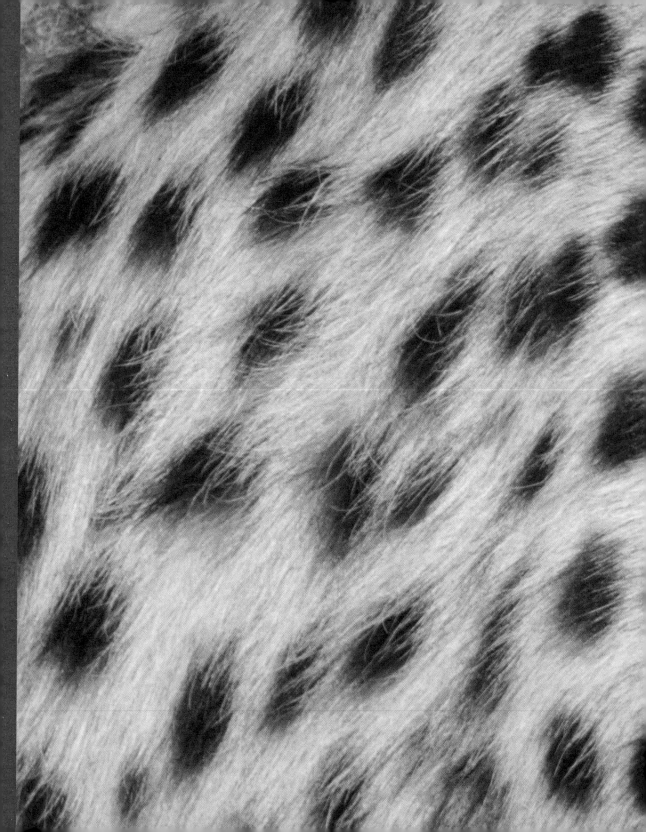

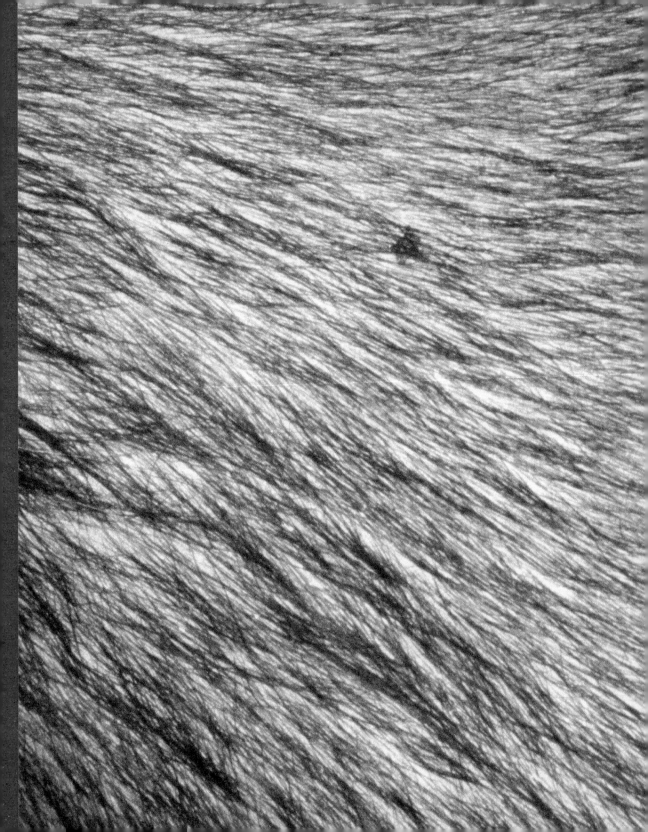

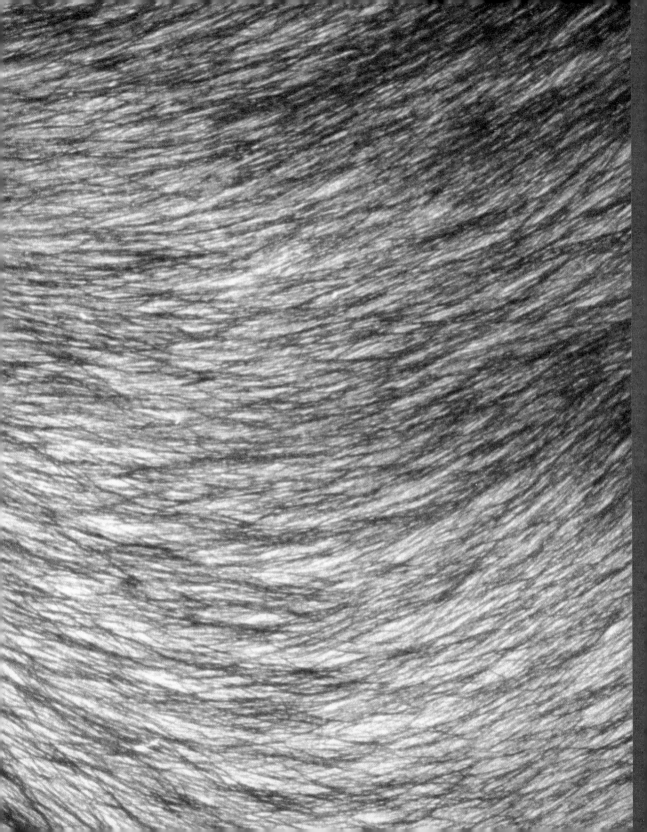

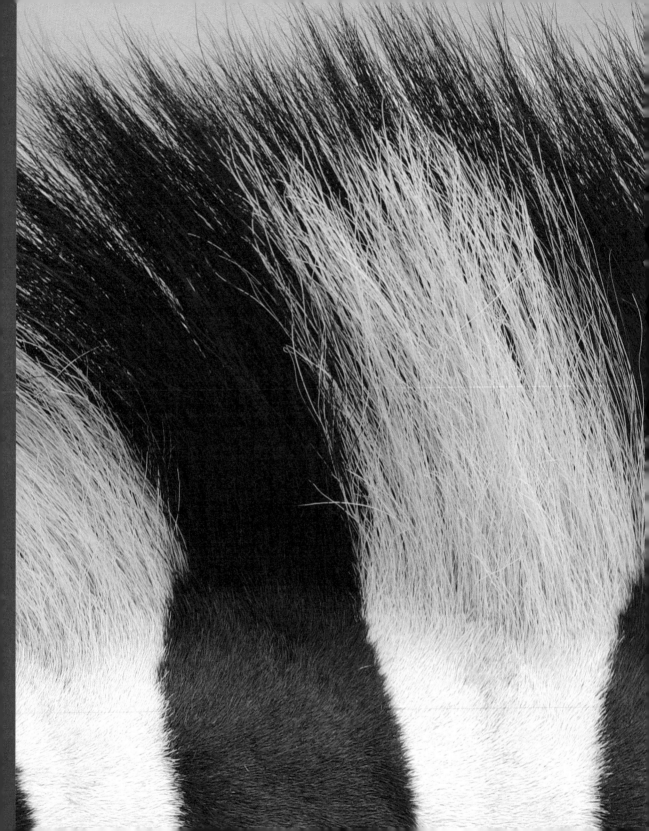

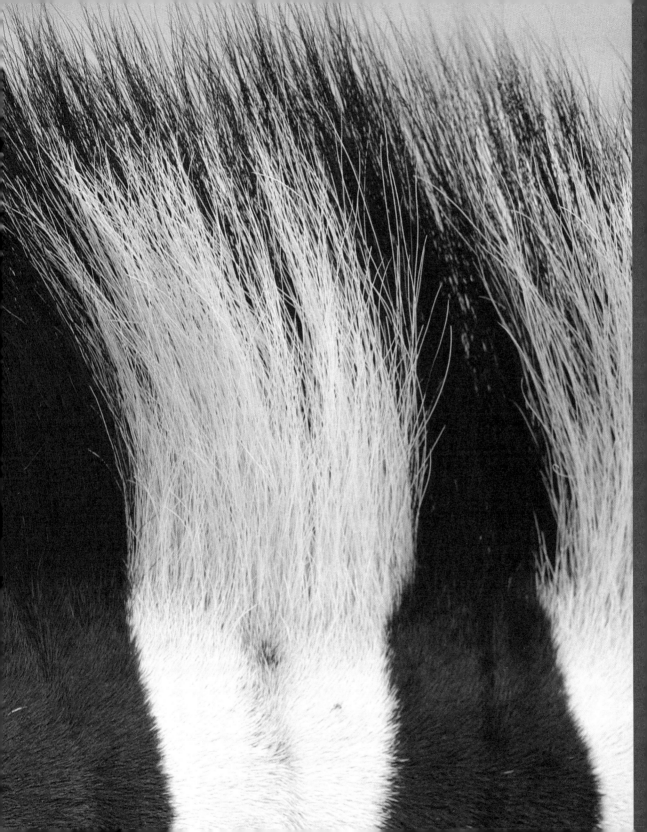

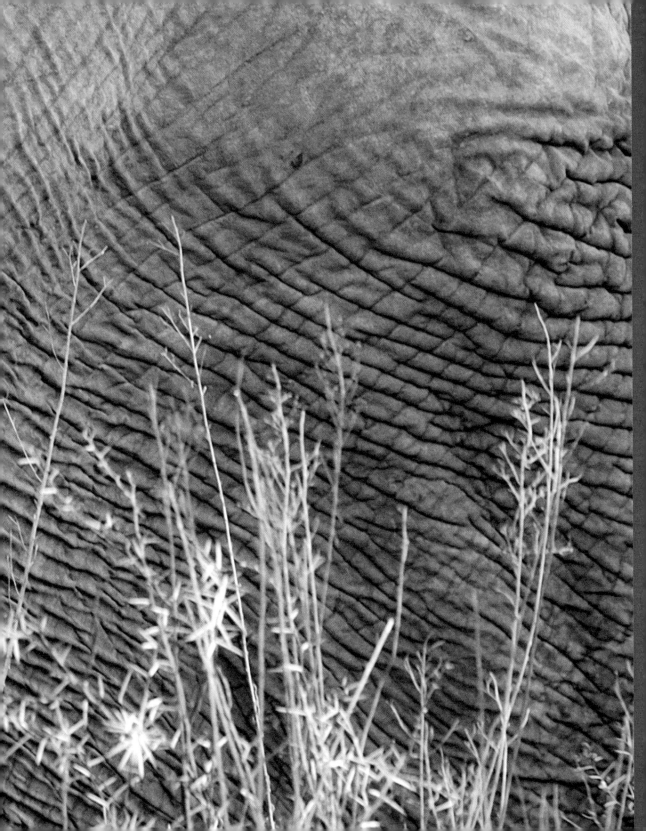

TO SHOW

TO YAWN

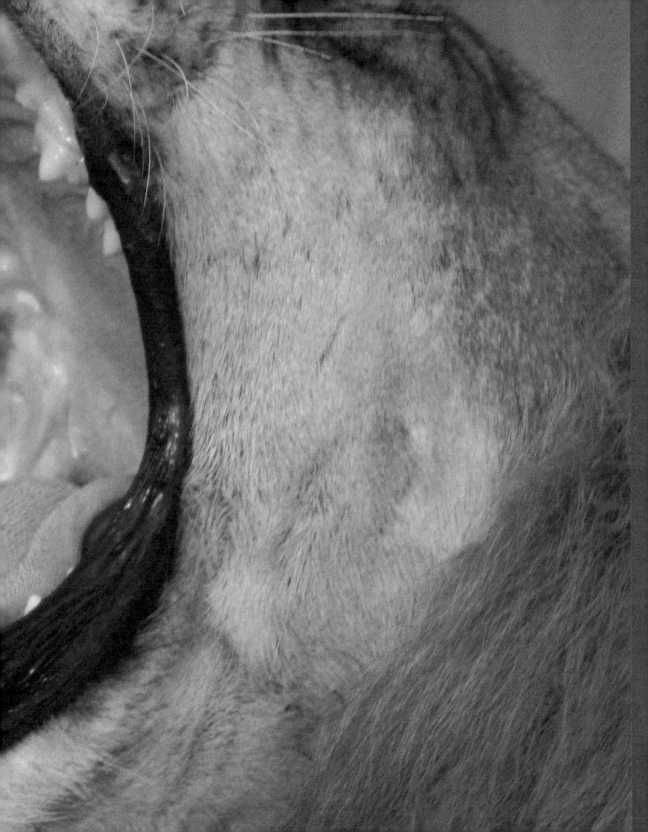

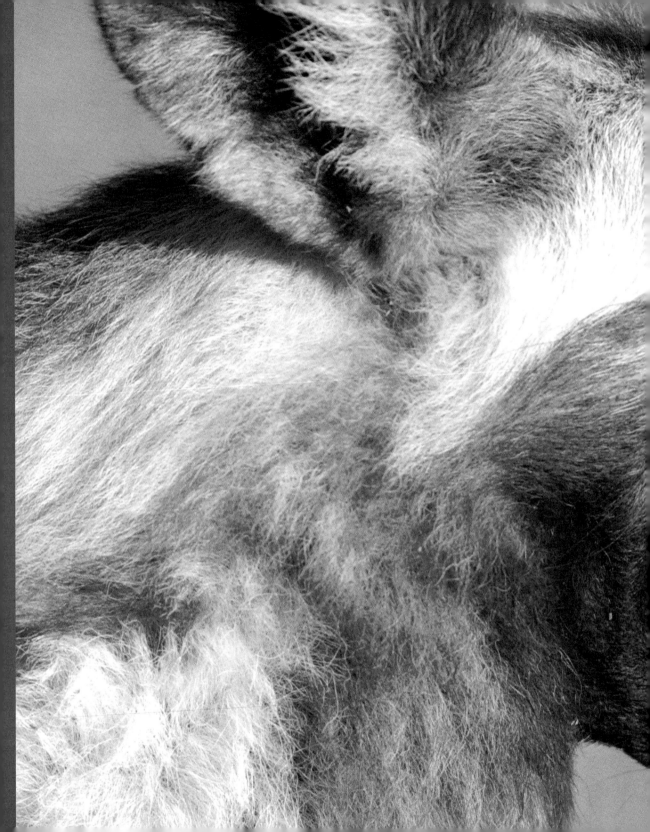

TO RELAX

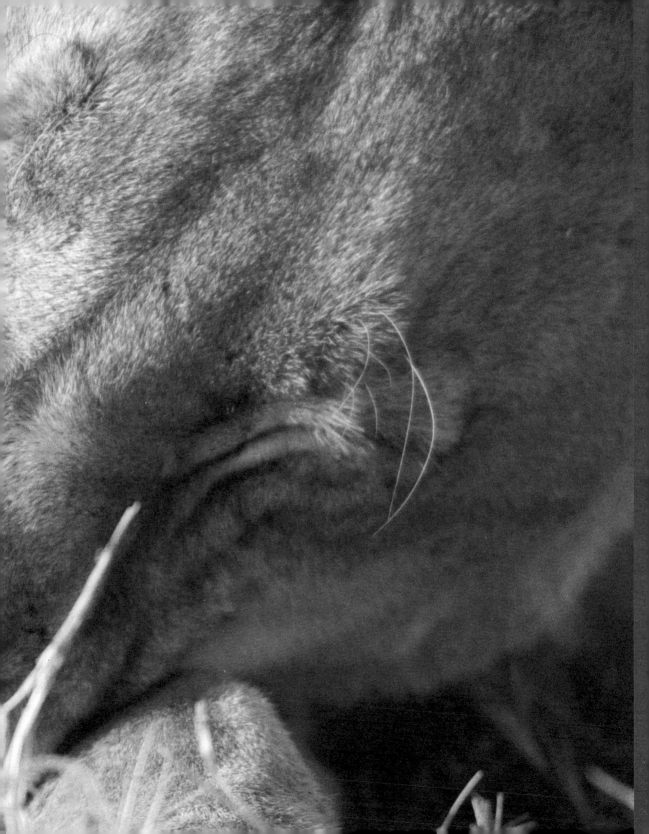

TO OBSERVE

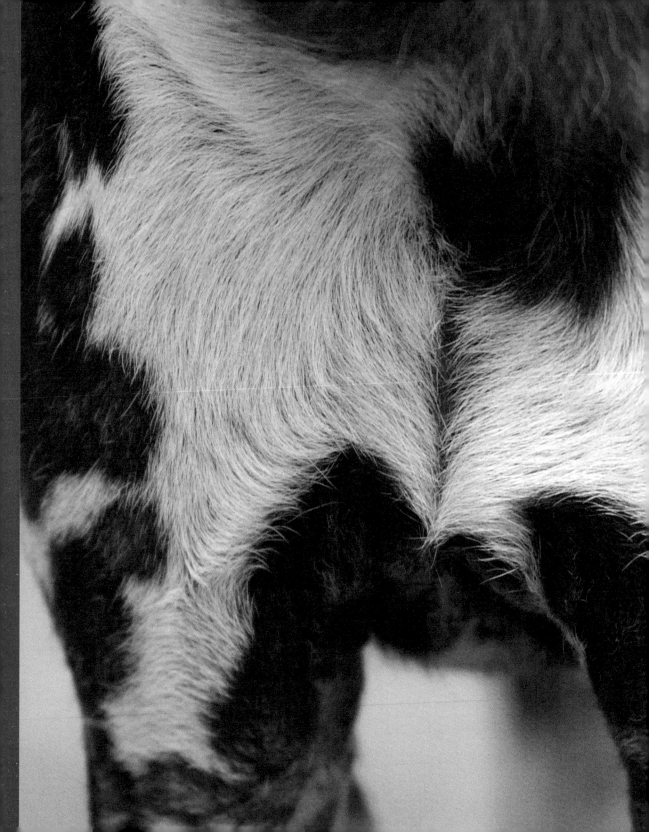

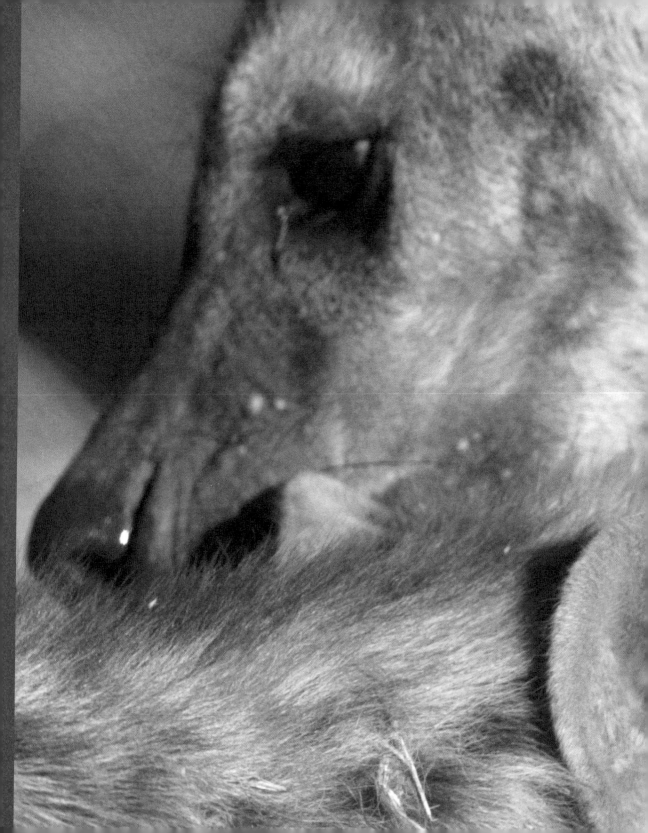

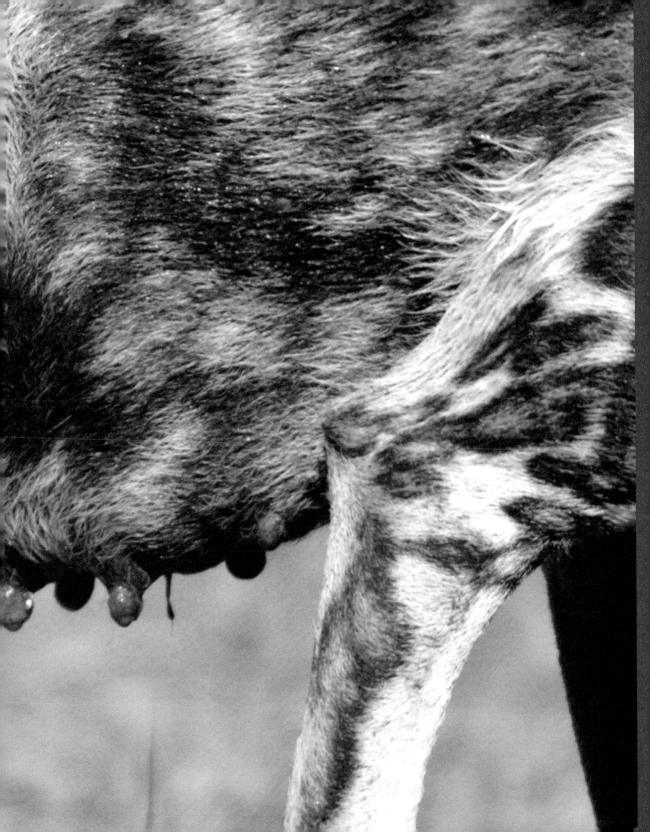

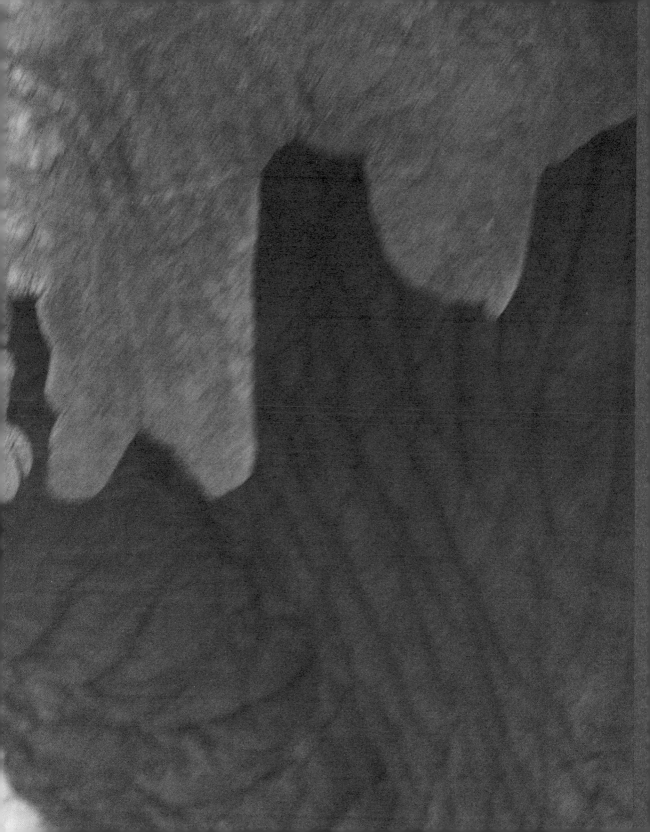

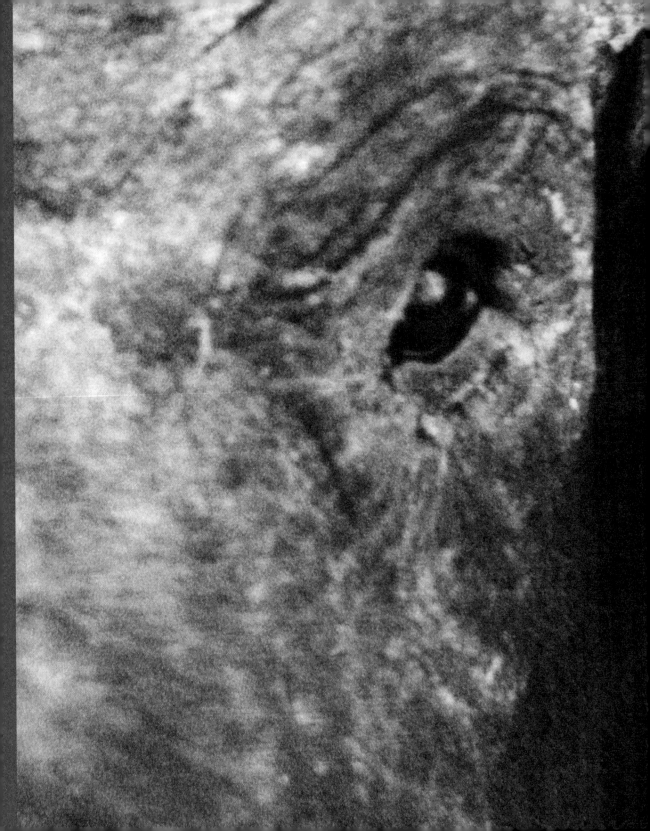

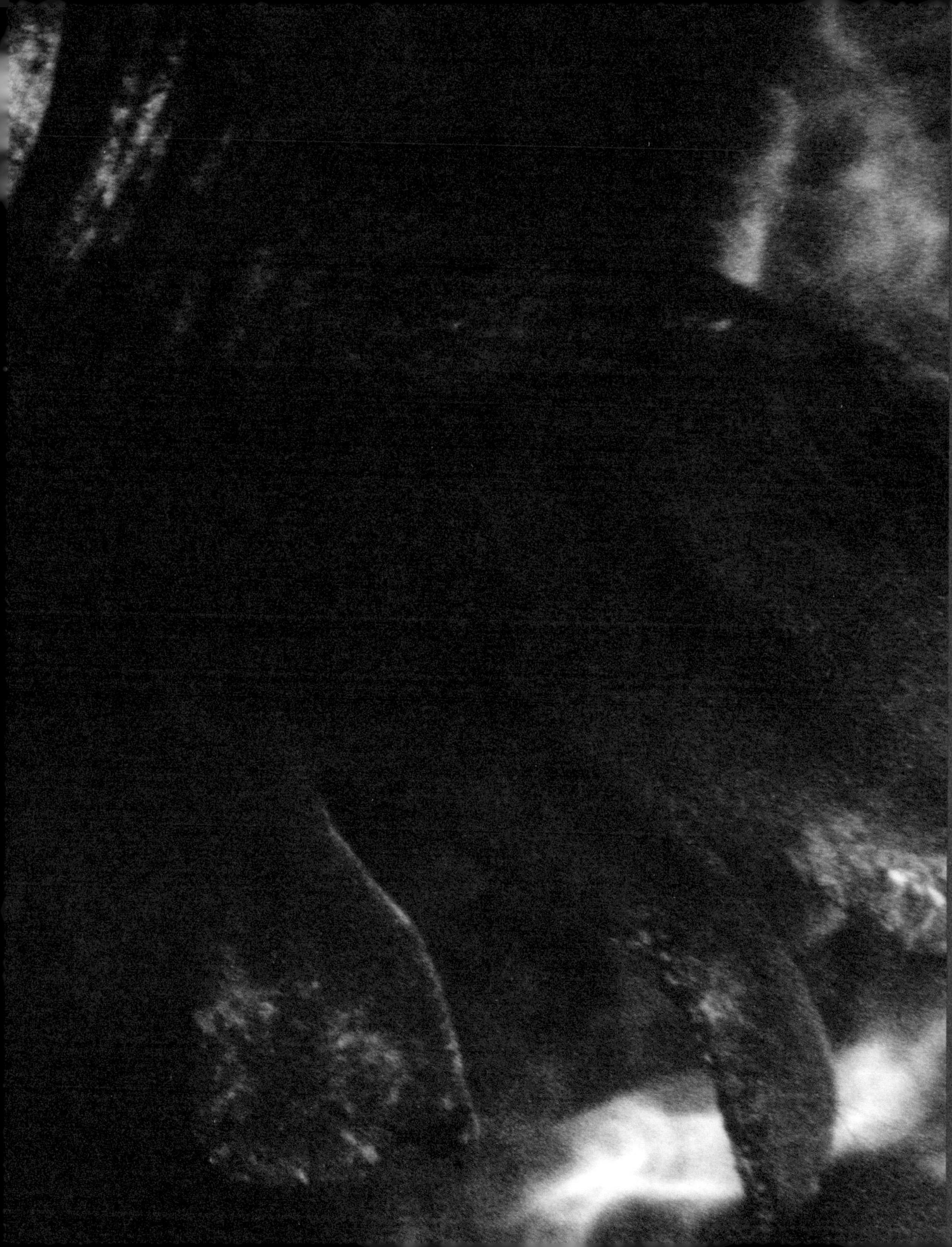

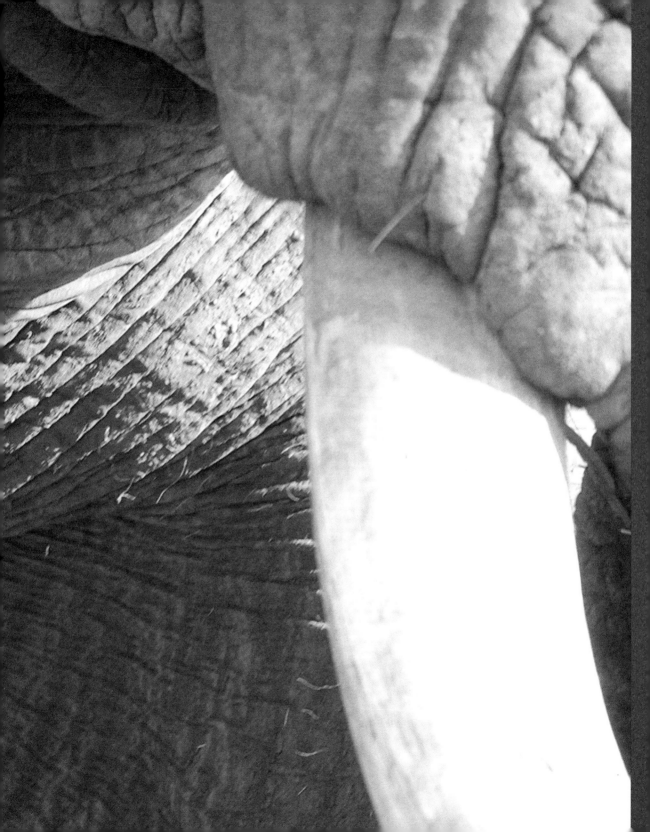

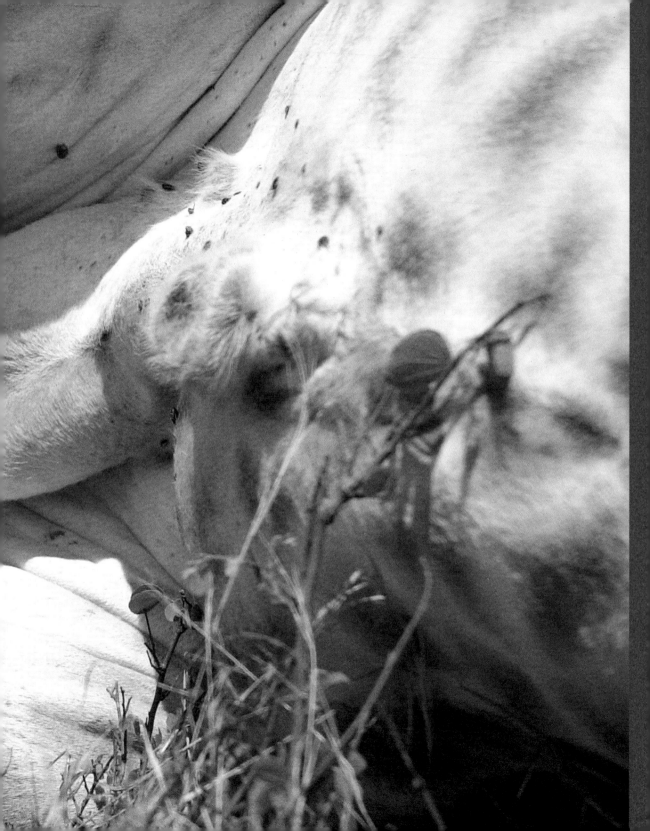

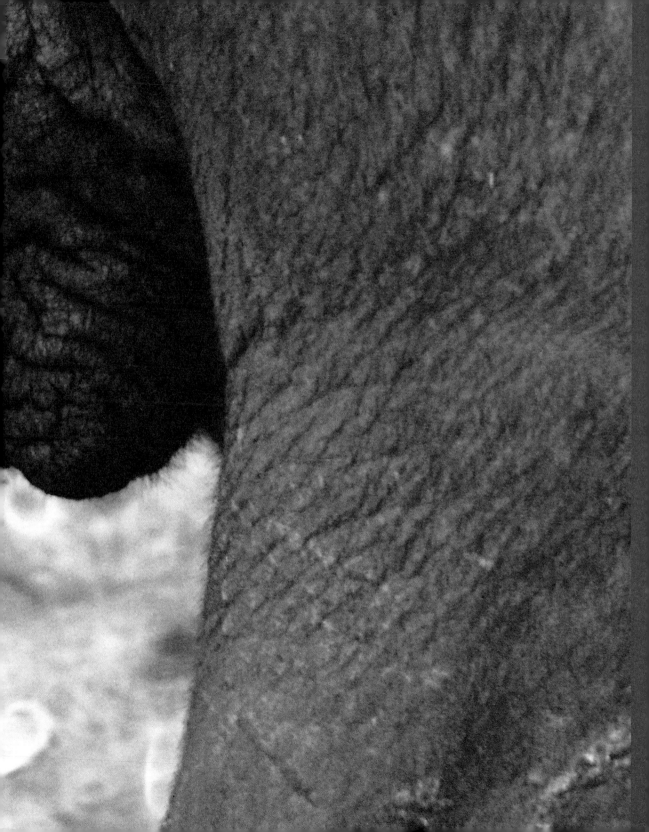

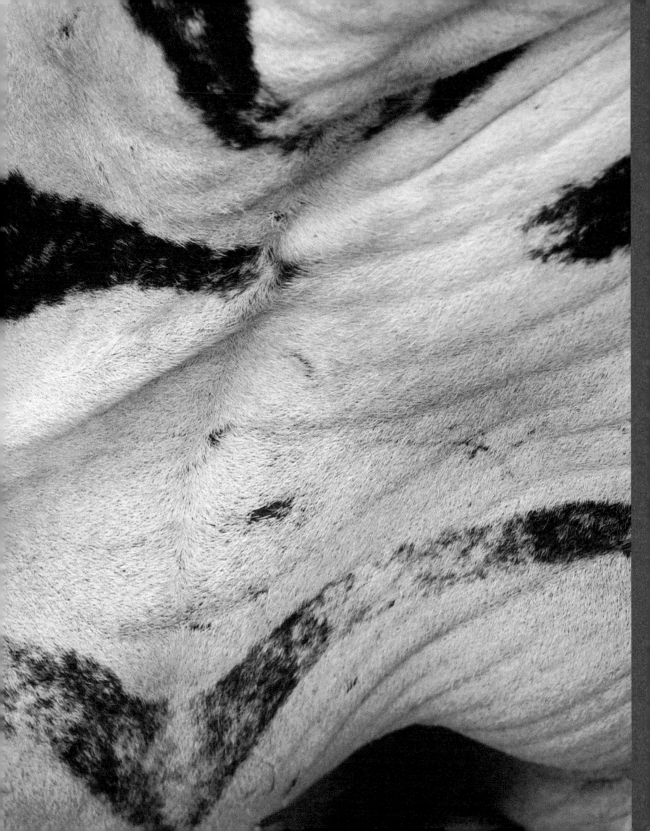

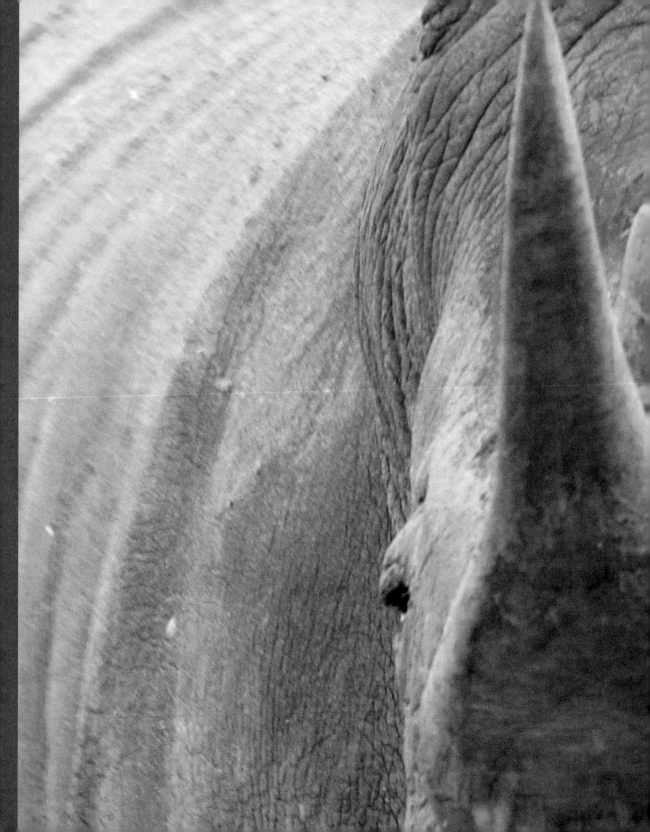

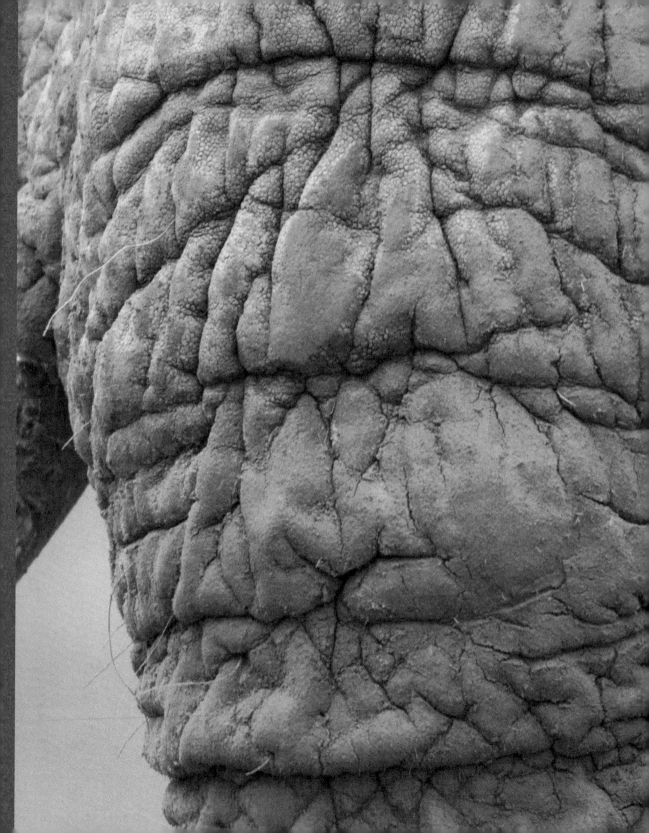

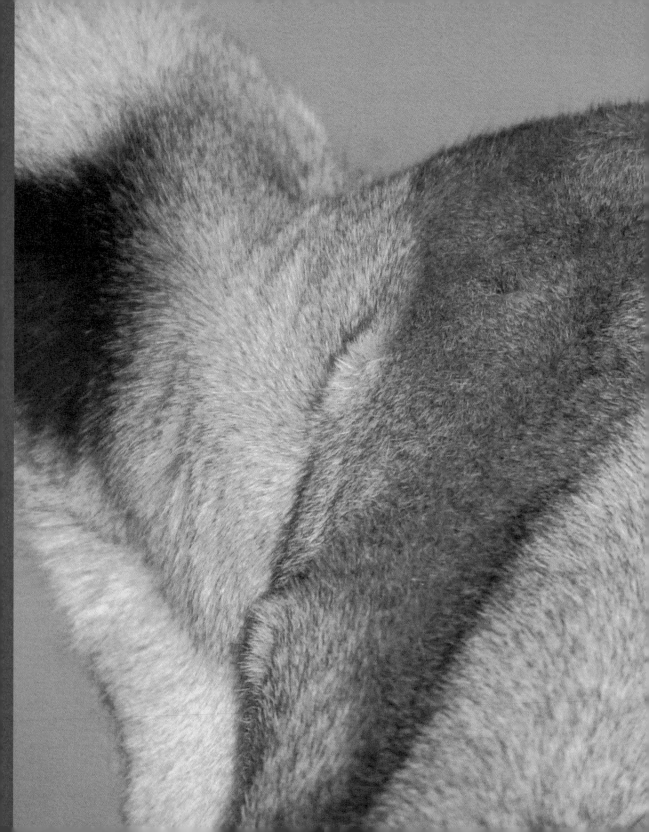

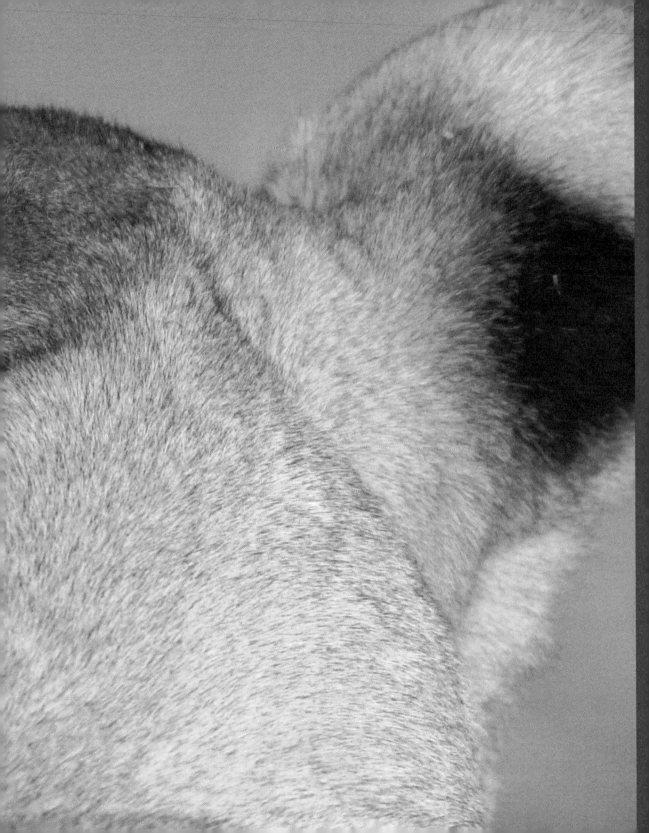

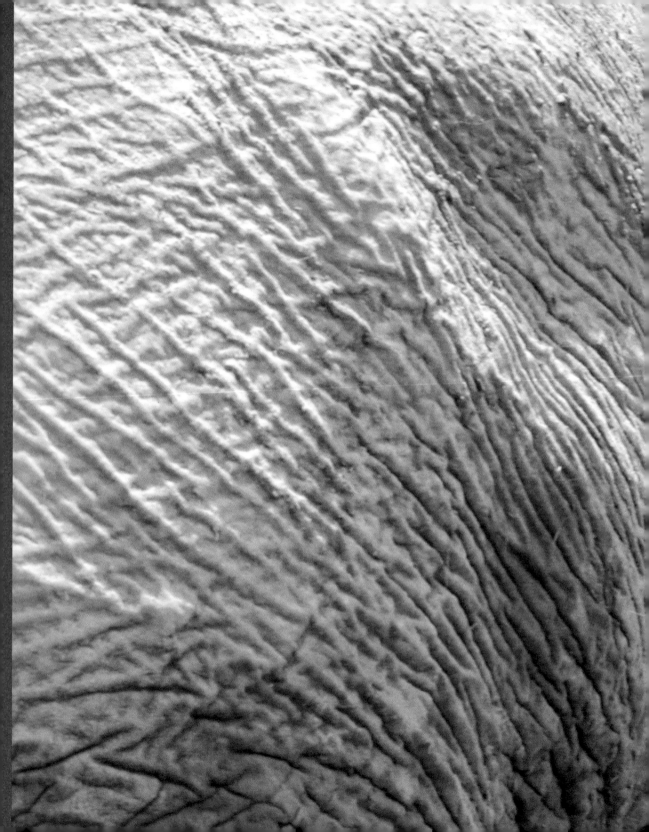

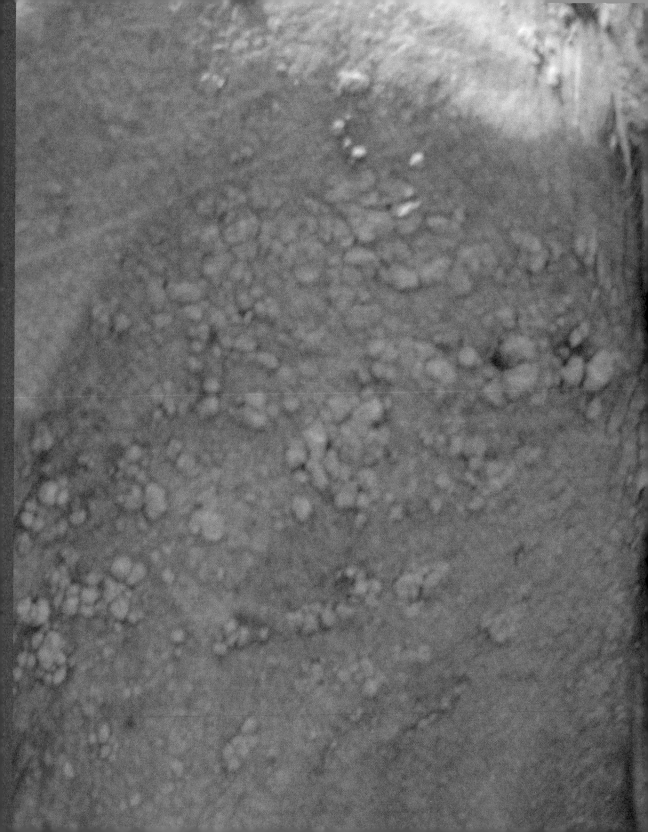

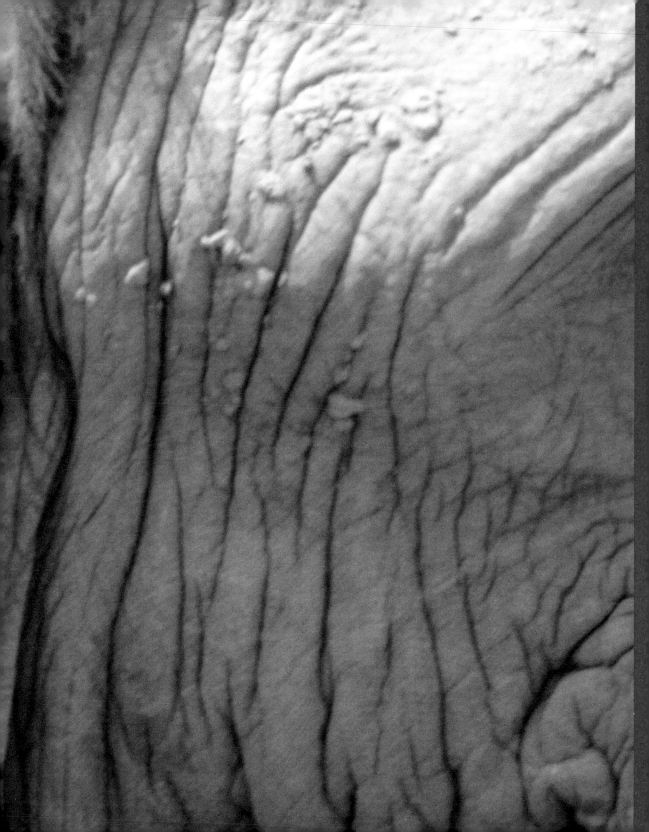

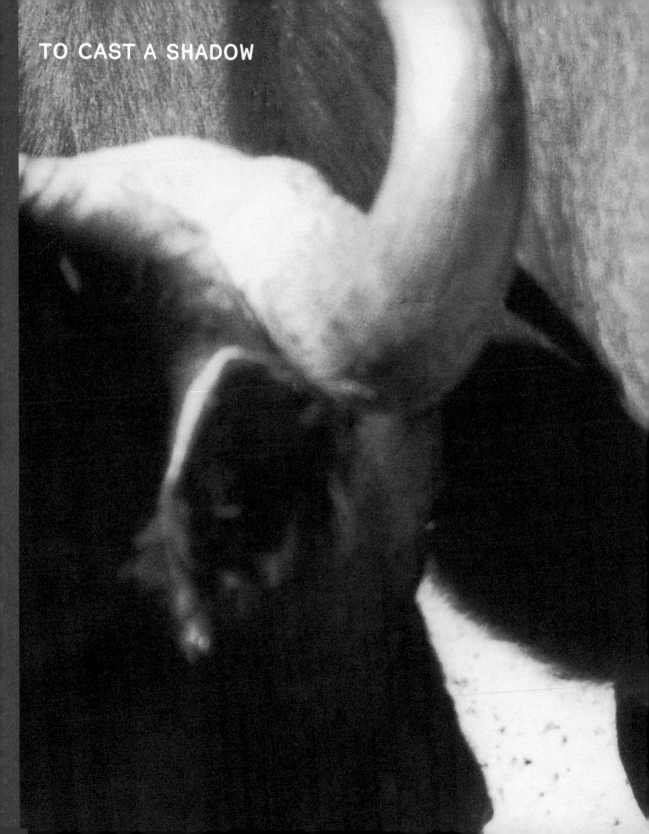

TO CAST A SHADOW

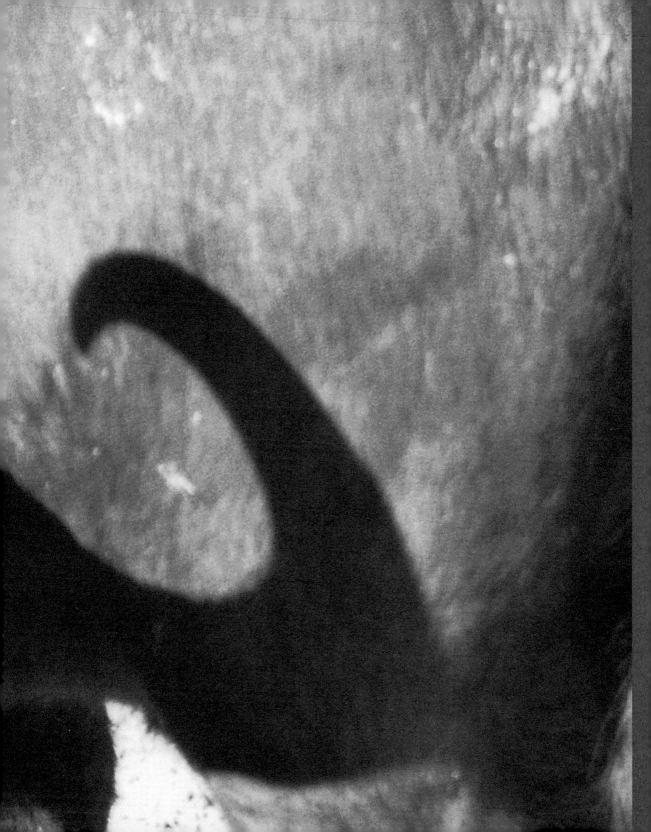

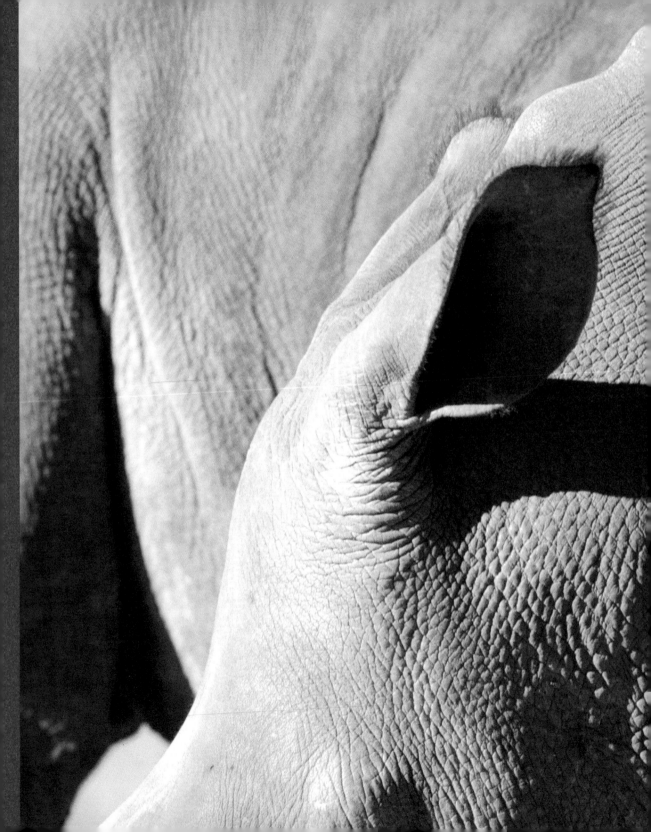

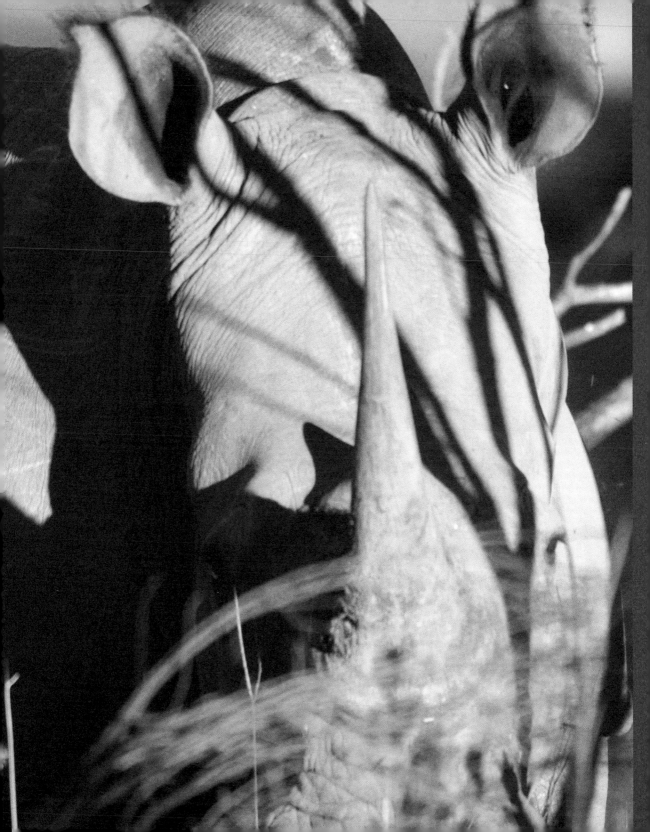

GOODBYE

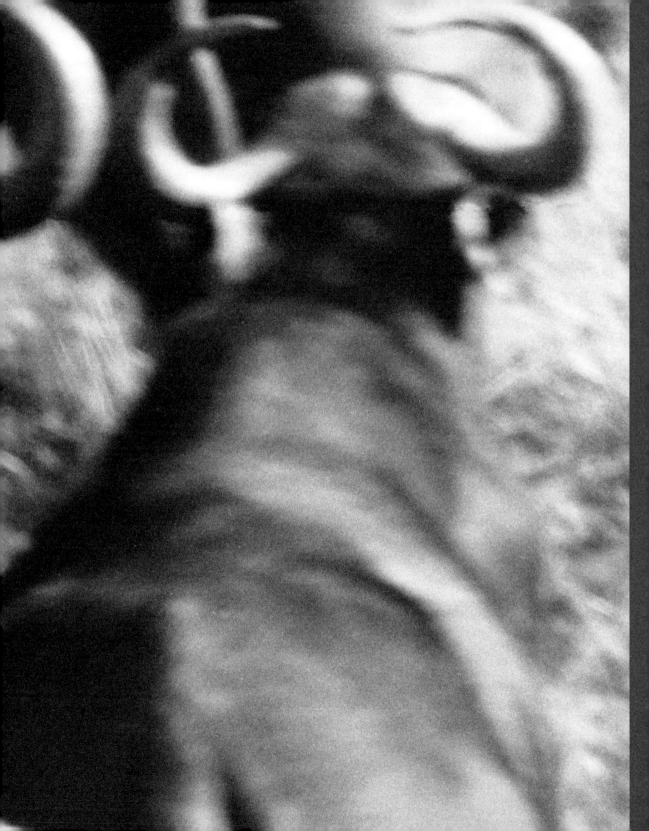

THE MEAN MAXIMUM AND MINIMUM AIR TEMPERATURE IN °C FOR THREE WEATHER STATIONS IN THE VICINITY OF THE STUDY AREA

Station	Blespaardspruit		Thabazimbi		Waterhoutboom	
Longitude	24°38'S		24°37'S		24°38'S	
Latitude	27°24'E		27°38'E		27°24'E	
Altitude	1 200 m		1 026 m		1 540 m	
Duration	4 y		47 y		7 y	
Daily Month	Daily Max	Daily Min	Daily Max	Daily Min	Daily Max	Daily Min
January	30.1	19.9	31.5	19.4	28.2	19.4
February	29.1	19.5	31.4	19.3	28.6	19.6
March	29.3	17.4	30.1	17.6	26.6	16.6
April	27.0	15.1	27.0	14.1	23.5	14.9
May	24.6	10.6	24.2	8.6	22.5	12.2
June	20.5	6.7	21.9	5.7	17.8	9.6
July	20.6	7.8	22.0	5.8	21.4	10.4
August	22.4	9.0	25.3	8.9	22.8	10.5
September	30.4	16.4	30.3	15.3	25.1	13.4
October	30.0	17.9	32.2	18.7	26.6	16.3
November	28.4	17.7	29.8	18.1	27.7	17.5
December	30.3	20.1	30.1	19.2	26.6	17.3

THE TOTAL ANNUAL RAINFALL (MM) FOR THREE WEATHER STATIONS IN THE VICINITY OF THE STUDY AREA

Station	Blespaardspruit	Thabazimbi	Waterhoutboom
Longitude	24°38'	24°37'	24°38'
Latitude	27°24'	27°24'	27°24'
Altitude	1 200 m	1 026 m	1 540 m
1977	–	840.5	–
1978	–	765.0	–
1979	–	666.0	–
1980	–	661.0	–
1981	–	553.5	–
1982	–	656.4	–
1983	–	554.1	–
1984	–	609.4	–
1985	–	504.2	–
1986	–	632.5	–
1987	–	577.5	–
1988	–	776.0	547.7
1989	–	672.5	671.8
1990	–	460.4	713.9
1991	429.2	924.0	464.6
1992	506.7	451.1	388.0
1993	566.1	706.1	550.7
1994	439.4	440.2	633.5
Mean	485.4	636.1	567.2

SOURCE: THE MARAKELE MANAGEMENT & DEVELOPMENT PLAN (2003) BY DR ANTHONY HALL-MARTIN

STATUS AND ESTIMATED PERFORMANCE OF HERBIVORE AND CARNIVORE SPECIES IN THE MARAKELE NATIONAL PARK
AND ESTIMATED QUALITY OF HABITAT

Species	Scientific name	Status[1]	Performance[2]	Habitat Quality[3]
HERBIVORES				
Aardvark	Orycteropus afer	PB	S?	G
Buffalo	Syncerus caffer	PB	U	G
Bushbuck	Tragelaphus scriptus	PB	S	G
Bushpig	Potamochoerus porcus	PB	S	G
Duiker Grey	Sylvicapra grimmia	PB	S	G
Eland	Taurotragus oryx	PB	U	G
Elephant	Loxodonta africana	PB	U	G
Gemsbok	Oryx gazella	PB	S/D	P
Giraffe	Giraffa camelopardalis	PC	U	G
Hartebeest Red	Alcelaphus buselaphus	PB	U	G
Hippopotamus	Hippopotamus amphibius	PC	U	G
Impala	Aepyceros melampus	PA	U	G
Klipspringer	Oreotragus oreotragus	PB	S?	G
Kudu	Tragelaphus strepsiceros	PA	U	G
Nyala	Tragelaphus angasi	PC#	U	M
Oribi	Ourebia ourebia	PH?		P (limited)
Reedbuck Common	Redunca arundinum	PB	D?	M (limited)
Reedbuck Mountain	Redunca fulvorufula	PB	S?	G
Rhebok Grey	Pelea capreolus	PC	S?	M
Rhinoceros Black	Diceros bicornis minor	PC	U	G
Rhinoceros White	Ceratotherium simum	PC	U	G
Roan Antelope	Hippotragus equinus	PC	D	P
Sable Antelope	Hippotragus niger	PB	D	P
Springbok	Antidorcas marsupialis	PH?	P	
Steenbok	Raphicerus campestris	PB	S	G
Tsessebe	Damaliscus lunatus	PB	U	G
Warthog	Phacochoerus africanus	PB	U	G
Waterbuck	Kobus ellipsiprymnus	PB	U	G
Wildebeest Blue	Connochaetes taurinus	PB	U	G
Zebra Plains	Equus quagga	PB	U	G
CARNIVORES				
Aardwolf	Proteles cristatus	PC	S?	G
African Wild Cat	Felis lybica	PB	S?	G
Caracal	Felis caracal	PB	S?	G
Cheetah	Acinonyx jubatus	PC	U	G
Honey Badger	Mellivora capensis	PC	S?	G
Hyaena Brown	Hyaena brunnea	PC	U	G
Hyaena Spotted	Crocuta crocuta	PH		G
Jackal Black-backed	Canis mesomelas	PB	U	G
Leopard	Panthera pardus	PC	U?	G
Lion	Panthera leo	PC		G
Serval	Felis serval	PC	?	M
African Wild Dog	Lycaon pictus	PC		G

1. Status: PA = population >250 individuals; PB = 25-250; PC = <25; PH = definite historical occurrence
   but not introduced as of yet: PH? = unconfirmed historical occurrence; # = extralimital species.
2. Population performance (up (U), stable (S) down (D), unsure(?))
3. Habitat quality (good (G), moderate (M), poor (P)).

YEAR AND SOURCE OF LARGE MAMMAL INTRODUCTIONS INTO MARAKELE NATIONAL PARK

Species	Year	No.	Source population
HERBIVORES			
Buffalo	1993	6	Addo Elephant NP
Buffalo	1993	10	Vaalbos NP
Buffalo	2002	30	Addo Elephant National Park
Buffalo	2003	30	Vaalbos National Park (Kwazulu and KNP stock)
Eland	1993	17	Rooipoort
Eland	1995	33	Vaalbos NP
Eland	2001	21	Vaalbos NP
Eland	2001	44	Independent Wildlife Services – Private farm Messina
Gemsbok	1994	30	Kalahari Gemsbok NP
Gemsbok	1996	9	Kalahari Gemsbok NP
Gemsbok	2001	50	Karoo National Park (35) and Vaalbos National Park (15)
Gemsbok	2001	13	Christoff Viljoen Capture
Elephants	1996	39	Kruger NP
Elephants	1999	12	Tuli, Botswana
Elephants	2001	21	Kruger NP
Giraffe	1996	25	Lowveld
Giraffe	2001	7	Specialist Game Services, Cullinan
Giraffe	2001	6	Independent Wildlife Services – Private farm Warmbaths
Giraffe	2002	2	Specialist Game Services, Cullinan
Hartebeest, red	1993	16	Vaalbos NP
Hartebeest, red	1994	11	Vaalbos NP
Hartebeest, red	1995	33	Vaalbos NP
Hartebeest, red	1996	14	Vaalbos NP
Hartebeest, red	2001	57	Vaalbos NP, Karoo National Park (40)
Hartebeest, red	2001	68	Specialist Game Services, Cullinan
Hartebeest, red	2001	28	Christoff Viljoen Capture
Hartebeest, red	2001	19	Independent Wildlife Services – Madikwe/Pilanesberg
Hippopotamus	1993	4	Kruger NP
Hippopotamus	2001	24	Lowveld
Hippopotamus	2002	3	Lowveld
Impala	2001	145	Specialist Game Services Cullinan
Impala	2001	44	Buchner Game Services
Impala	2001	29	Independent Wildlife Services – Madikwe/Pilanesberg
Impala	2002	59	Independent Wildlife Services – Private farm Alldays
Kudu	2001	18	Specialist Game Services
Reedbuck, common	1990	22	St Lucia
Reedbuck, common	1991	9	Dullstroom
Reedbuck, common	2001	36	Independent Wildlife Services – Weenen region Kwazulu Natal
Rhinoceros, black	1993	1	Kruger NP
Rhinoceros, black	1993	1	Zululand
Rhinoceros, black	1993	3	Kruger NP
Rhinoceros, black	1996	4	Kwazulu-Natal
Rhinoceros, black	1996	4	Kruger NP
Rhinoceros, white	1994	12	Kruger NP
Rhinoceros, white	1995	4	Kruger NP
Rhinoceros, white	1996	1	Kruger NP
Rhinoceros, white	2001	24	Kruger NP
Roan antelope	1995	10	Sable Ranch, ex Namibia
Sable antelope	1997	10	Lowveld
Tsessebe	1993	43	Doringdraaidam
Tsessebe	1993	16	Doringdraaidam
Tsessebe	2001	12	Specialist Game Services
Waterbuck	2001	57	Specialist Game Services
Wildebeest, blue	1994	13	Vaalbos NP, Rooipoort
Wildebeest, blue	1995	13	Vaalbos NP, Rooipoort
Wildebeest, blue	1996	30	Vaalbos NP
Wildebeest, blue	1996	16	Kalahari Gemsbok NP
Wildebeest, blue	2001	40	Vaalbos NP
Wildebeest, blue	2001	85	Specialist Game Services, Cullinan
Wildebeest, blue	2001	5	Independent Wildlife Services – Madikwe/Pilanesberg
Zebra, plains	1994	123	Kruger NP
Zebra, plains	1996	144	Kruger NP
Zebra, plains	2001	15	Buchner Game Services
Zebra, plains	2001	109	Specialist Game Services, Tuli GR
Zebra, plains	2001	190	Independent Wildlife Services – Madikwe/Pilanesberg

CARNIVORES
Wild Dogs	2001	5	Northern Province, Botswana
Wild Dogs	2002	3	Botswana
Lions	2003	<5	Pilanesberg/Madikwe – Etosha NP
Spotted Hyaena	2002	<10	Kruger National Park
Cheetah	2003	<5	Local sources

LARGE MAMMAL STOCKING RATE FOR THE LOWLAND BUSHVELD, MID SLOPES AND UPLAND AREAS IN MARAKELE NATIONAL PARK
CURRENT POPULATION ESTIMATES ARE BASED ON UNCORRECTED FIGURES FROM AN AERIAL SURVEY UNDERTAKEN IN SEPTEMBER 2002

Group Species	Recommended maximum numbers per habitat			Maximum numbers recommended	Marakele Park PTY population	MNP population	MNP total population	
	Lowlands	Midslopes	Uplands					
BULK GRAZERS								
White Rhino	71	15	66	152	31	30	61	
Buffalo	122		25	98	245	13	0	13
Roan	72	15	41	128	0	0	0	
Sable	93	19	471	59	1	12	13	
Zebra	208	43	166	417	418	142	560	
Waterbuck	92	19	146	257	116	8	124	
Hippo	20	4	0	24	14	0	14	
CONCENTRATE								
Blue Wildebeest	377	78	313	768	527	122	649	
Gemsbok	322	67	112	501	45	8	53	
Red Hartebeest	254	53	423	730	141	17	158	
Tsessebe	413	86	165	664	19	64	83	
C. Reedbuck	163	34	130	327	3	3	6	
Warthog	302	63	482	847	792	185	977	
Mt Reedbuck	188	39	125	352	0	9	9	
MIXED								
Elephant	87	18	69	174	63	0	63	
Eland	174	36	259	469	96	14	110	
Impala	702	145	879	1726	1335	377	1712	
Ostrich	372	77	330	779	12	14	26	
BROWSERS								
Black Rhino	53	11	8	72	6	11	17	
Giraffe	50	10	20	80	14	22	36	
Kudu	291	60	77	428	242	119	361	
Bushbuck	181	38	48	267	26	9	35	
Nyala	52	11	14	77	6	4	10	
Duiker	109	23	29	161	2	4	6	
Steenbok	109	23	29	161	2	5	7	
Grey Rhebok	60	13	16	89	0	0	0	
CARNIVORES*								
Lions	10	2	8	20	1	0	1	
Spotted Hyaena	12	3	10	25	4	0	4	
Wild Dog	8	2	8	18	6	8	24	
Cheetah	10	2	8	20	8	?	8	
Brown Hyaena				24	?	?	?	
Leopard				14	?	?	?	
TOTAL								
HERBIVORES	4938	1023	4092	10052	3924	1179	5103	
CARNIVORES	33	12	39	120	29?	8	37?	

* Leopard, brown hyena cheetah are all resident, but numbers not yet quantified. The fence removal between
  Marakele/Welgevonden will increase lion numbers. Further introductions in progress. (PvV)

RED DATA LARGE MAMMAL SPECIES OCCURRING OR EXPECTED TO OCCUR IN MARAKELE NATIONAL PARK

Category	MAMMALS	
ENDANGERED	Roan Antelope	Hippotragus equinus
	African Wild Dog	Lycaon pictus
VULNERABLE	Honey Badger	Mellivora capensis
	African Wild Cat	Felis lybica
	Pangolin	Manis temminckii
	Black Rhino	Diceros bicornis minor
	Sable Antelope	H. niger niger
	Aardvark	Orycteropus afer
	Cheetah	Acinonyx jubatus
RARE	Hedgehog	Atelerix frontalis
	African Weasel	Poecilogale albinucha
	African Civet	Civettictis civetta australis
	Aardwolf	Proteles cristatus
	Brown Hyaena	Hyaena brunnea
	Serval	Felis serval
	Leopard	Panthera pardus
	Hippopotamus	Hippopotamus amphibius
	Tsessebe	Damaliscus lunatus
ENDEMIC	Grey Rhebok	Pelea capreolus

BIRD SPECIES OF CONSERVATION CONCERN THAT OCCUR IN MARAKELE NATIONAL PARK

Species both globally and nationally threatened
* Species does not meet IBA threshold

		Breeding (pairs)	Total numbers
GLOBALLY THREATENED			
Gyps coprotheres	Cape Vulture	700–900	1800–2200
Falco naumanni*	Lesser Kestrel		OV
Anthropoides paradisea	Blue Crane	Br	30–60
NATIONALLY THREATENED			
Gorsachius leuconotus	White-backed Night Heron	5–10	10–30
Gyps africanus	White-backed Vulture	20–30	50–100
Torgos tracheliotus*	Lappet-faced Vulture		2–3
Aquila rapax	Tawny Eagle	4–5	10–15
Polemaetus bellicosus	Martial Eagle	2–3	6–10
Terathopius ecaudatus*	Bateleur		OV
	African Finfoot	10–15	20–30
Neotis denhami	Denham's (Stanley's) Bustard		10–20
Eupodites [s.] barrowii (cafra)	Barrow's (White-bellied) Korhaan	Br?	10–15
Tyto capensis	African Grass Owl	1–2	2–10
Bucorvus leadbeateri*	Ground Hornbill	Br?	4–8
GLOBALLY NEAR-THREATENED			
Oenanthe bifasciata	Buff-streaked Chat	Br	200–500
NATIONALLY NEAR-THREATENED			
Ciconia nigra*	Black Stork	2–3	5–8
Sagittarius serpentarius	Secretary Bird	15–30	30–80
Falco peregrinus	Peregrine Falcon	5–10	10–30
Falco biarmicus	Lanner Falcon	20–40	50–100
Rostratula benghalensis*	Greater Painted-snipe (Painted Snipe)		OV
Alcedo semitorquata	Half-collared Kingfisher	30–50	60–120

RR & BRA		**STATUS**
Turdus libonyanus	Kurrichane Thrush	Abundant
Oenanthe bifasciata	Buff-streaked Chat	Uncommon
Cossypha humeralis	White-throated Robin-Chat	Fairly Common
Cercotrichas (Erythropygia) paena	Kalahari Scrub-Robin (Kalahari Robin)	Uncommon
Calamonastes (Camaroptera) fasciolatus	Barred Wren-Warbler (African Barred Warbler)	Common
Lamprotornis australis	Burchell's Starling	Common
Promerops gurneyi	Gurney's Sugarbird	Uncommon
Cinnyris (Nectarinia) talatala	White-bellied Sunbird	Common

RR & BRA = Restricted-range and biome-restricted assemblage
Br = Confirmed breeding
Br? = Suspected breeding
OV = Occasional visitor

IMPORTANT ECOLOGICAL PROCESSES OPERATING WITHIN THE MARAKELE NATIONAL PARK CRITICAL TO THE CONSERVATION OF BIODIVERSITY

Primary level	Process	Operator
Landscape	Upland-Lowland gradient	
	Upland-Lowland interfaces	
	Vegetation unit interfaces	
	Riverine corridors	
	Natural fire regimes	
	Productivity gradients	
	Vegetation dynamics (succession)	
Species	Trophic level	Bulk grazing
		Concentrate grazing
		Mixed feeding
		Browsing
		Scavenging
		Predation
	Transportation	Seed dispersal
		Nutrient dispersal
	Habitat architecture	Structural change
		Grazing lawns
		Path opening
	Bioperturbation	Wallowing
		Digging
		Hoof action
		Geophagy
		River beds
		Dust bathing
		Burrowing
	Other processes	Litter production
		Germination
Population	Genetic viability	Miminum Viable Populations (MVPs)
	Parasitism	
	Epidemiology	

RSA = Endemic to the RSA
SA = Endemic to the southern African subregion

ORDER INSECTIVORA
Family Soricidae

	Shrews		
Myosorex varius	Forest Shrew	Bosskeerbek	RSA
Suncus lixus	Great Dwarf Shrew	Groter Dwergskeerbek	SA
Suncus varilla	Lesser Dwarf Shrew	Kleiner Dwergskeerbek	SA
Suncus infinitesimus	Least Dwarf Shrew	Kleinste Dwergskeerbek	RSA
Crocidura mariquensis	Swamp Musk Shrew	Vleiskeerbek	SA
Crocidura fuscomurina	Tiny Musk Shrew	Dwergskeerbek	
Crocidura cyanea	Reddish-grey Musk Shrew	Rooigrysskeerbek	
Crocidura silacea	Peters' Musk Shrew	Peters se Skeerbek	SA
Crocidura hirta	Lesser Red Musk Shrew	Klein Rooiskeerbek	

Family Erinaceidae

	Hedgehogs	
Atilerix frontalis	South African Hedgehog	Suid-Afrikaanse krimpvarkie

ORDER MACROSCELIDEA
Family Macroscelididae

	Elephant-shrews	
Elephantulus brachyrhynchus	Short-snouted Elephant Shrew	Kortneus Klaasneus
Elephantulus myurus	Rock Elephant Shrew	Klipklaasneus

ORDER CHIROPTERA — Bats
SUB-ORDER MEGACHIROPTERA — Fruit-eating Bats
Family Pteropodidae

	Fruit bats	
Eidolon helvum	Straw-coloured Fruit Bat	Geel Vrugtevlermuis

SUB-ORDER MICROCHIROPTERA — Insect-eating Bats
Family Emballonuridae

	Sheath-tailed Bats	
Taphozous mauritianus	Tomb Bat	Witlyf Vlermuis

Family Molossidae

	Free-tailed Bats		
Sauromys petrophilus	Flat-headed Free-tailed Bat	Platkop-losstertvlermuis	SA
Tadarida aegyptiaca	Egyptian Free-tailed Bat	Egiptiese losstertvlermuis	

Family Vespertilionidae

	Vesper Bats		
Miniopterus schreibersii	Schreibers' Long-fingered Bat	Schreibers se Grotvlermuis	
Myotis welwitschii	Welwitsch's hairy Bat	Welwitsch se Langhaarvlermuis	SA
Myotis tricolor	Temminck's hairy Bat	Temminck se Langhaar Vlermuis	
Pipistrellus kuhlii	Kuhl's Bat	Kuhl se Vlermuis	
Pipistrellus rusticus	Rusty Bat	Roeskleurvlermuis	
Neuromicia zuluensis	Aloe Serotine Bat	Aalwyn Dakvlermuis	
Neuromicia capensis	Cape Serotine Bat	Kaapse Dakvlermuis	
Scotophilus dinganii	Yellow House Bat	Geel Dakvlermuis	
Scotophilus viridis	Lesser Yellow House Bat	Klein Geelvlermuis	
Nycticeinops schlieffenii	Schlieffen's Bat	Schlieffen se Vlermuis	

Family Nycteridae

	Slit-faced Bats	
Nycteris thebaica	Common Slit-faced Bat	Gewone Spleetneusvlermuis

Family Rhinolophidae

	Horseshoe Bats	
Rhinolophus hildebrandtii	Hildebrandt's Horseshoe Bat	Hildebrandt se Saalneusvlermuis
Rhinolophus clivosus	Geoffroy's Horseshoe Bat	Geoffroy se Saalneusvlermuis
Rhinolophus darlingi	Darling's Horseshoe Bat	Darling se Saalneusvlermuis
Rhinolophus blasii	Peak-saddle Horseshoe Bat	Spitssaalneusvlermuis
Rhinolophus simulator	Bushveld Horseshoe Bat	Bosveld Saalneusvlermuis

Family Hipposideridae

	Trident and Leaf-nosed Bats	
Hipposideros caffer	Sundevall's Leaf-nosed Bat	Sundevall se Bladneusvlermuis
Cloeotis percivali	Short-eared Trident Bat	Drietand-bladneusvlermuis

ORDER PRIMATES — Bushbabies, Baboons and Monkeys
SUB-ORDER STREPSIRRHINI
Family Galagonidae

	Bushbabies	
Galago moholi	South African Lesser Bushbaby	Nagapie

Family Cercopithecidae

	Monkeys and Baboons	
Papio hamadryas	Chacma Baboon	Kaapse Bobbejaan
Cercopithecus aethiops	Vervet Monkey	Blouaap

ORDER PHOLIDOTA   Pangolin
Family Manidae
Manis temminckii   Pangolin   Ietermagog

ORDER LAGOMORPHA   Hares and Rabbits
Family Leporidae   Hares, Rock Rabbits, Rabbits
Lepus saxatilis   Scrub Hare   Kolhaas
Pronolagus randensis   Jameson's Red Rabbit   Jameson se Rooiklipkonyn   SA

ORDER RODENTIA   Rodents
Family Bathyergidae   Molerats
Cryptomys hottentotus   Common Molerat   Vaalmol

Family Hystricidae   Porcupinnes
Hystrix africaeaustralis   Cape Porcupine   Kaapse Ystervark

Family Pedetidae   Springhares
Pedetes capensis   Springhare   Springhaas

Family Myoxidae   Dormice
Graphiurus platyops   Rock Dormouse   Klipwaaierstertmuis
Graphiurus murinus   Woodland Dormouse   Boswaaierstertmuis

Family Sciuridae   Squirrels
Xerus inauris   Cape Ground Squirrel   Waaierstertgrondeekhoring   SA
Paraxerus cepapi   Tree Squirrel   Boomeekhoring

Family Thryonomyidae   Canerats
Thryonomys swinderianus   Greater Canerat   Groot Rietrot   RSA

Family Muridae   Rats and Mice
Otomys angoniensis   Angoni Vlei Rat   Angoni-vleirot   SA
Otomys irroratus   Vlei Rat   Vleirot   SA
Acomys spinosissimus   Spiny Mouse   Stekelmuis
Lemniscomys rosalia   Single-striped Mouse   Eenstreepmuis
Rhabdomys pumilio   Striped Mouse   Streepmuis
Dasymus incomtus   Water Rat   Waterrot
Mus indutus   Desert Pygmy Mouse   Woestyndwergmuis
Mus minutoides   Pygmy Mouse   Dwergmuis
Mastomys natalensis   Natal Multimammate Mouse   Natalse Vaalveldmuis
Mastomys coucha   Multimammate Mouse   Vaalveldmuis   SA
Thallomys paedulcus   Tree Rat   Boomrot
Aethomys namaquensis   Namaqua Rock Mouse   Namakwalandse Klipmuis
Aethomys chrysophilus   Red Veld Rat   Afrikaanse Bosrot
Rattus rattus   House Rat   Huisrot
Gerbillurus paeba   Hairy-footed Gerbil   Haarpootnagmuis
Tatera leucogaster   Bushveld Gerbil   Bosveldse nagmuis
Tatera brantsii   Highveld Gerbil   Hoëveldse nagmuis
Saccostomys campestris   Pouched Mouse   Wangsakmuis
Dendromus melanotis   Grey Climbing Mouse   Grysklimmuis
Dendromus mystacalis   Chestnut Climbing Mouse   Roeskleurklimmuis
Steatomys pratensis   Fat Mouse   Vetmuis
Steatomys krebsii   Krebs's Fat Mouse   Krebs se Vetmuis

ORDER CARNIVORA
Family Hyaenidae   Aardwolves, Hyaenas
Proteles cristatus   Aardwolf   Aardwolf
Parahyaena brunnea   Brown Hyaena   Strandjut
Crocuta crocuta   Spotted Hyaena   Gevlekte Hiëna

Family Felidae   Cats
Acinonyx jubatus   Cheetah   Jagluiperd
Panthera pardus   Leopard   Luiperd
Panthera leo   Lion   Leeu
Caracal caracal   Caracal   Rooikat
Felis silvestris lybica   African Wild Cat   Vaalboskat
Leptailurus serval   Serval   Tierboskat

Family Canidae   Foxes, Wild Dogs and Jackals
Otocyon megalotis   Bat-eared Fox   Bakoorvos
Vulpes chama   Cape Fox   Silwervos
Canis mesomelas   Black-backed Jackal   Rooijakkals

Family Mustelidae	Otters, Polecats, Weasels, Honey Badgers		
Aonyx capensis	Cape Clawless Otter	Groototter	
Mellivora capensis	Honey Badger	Ratel	
Poecilogale albinucha	African Weasel	Slangmuishond	SA
Ictonyx striatus	Striped Polecat	Stinkmuishond	

Family Viverridae	Civets, Genets and Surate		
Civettictis civetta	African Civet	Afrikaanse Siwet	
Genetta genetta	Small-spotted Genet	Kleinkolmuskejaatkat	
Genetta tigrina	Large-spotted Genet	Rooikolmuskejaatkat	

Family Herpestidae	Mongooses		
Paracynictis selousi	Selous' Mongoose	Kleinwitstertmuishond	
Cynictis penicillata	Yellow Mongoose	Witkwasmuishond	
Galerella sanguinea	Slender Mongoose	Swartkwasmuishond	
Ichneumia albicauda	White-tailed Mongoose	Witstertmuishond	
Atilax paludinosus	Water Mongoose	Kommetjiegatmuishond	
Mungos mungo	Banded Mongoose	Gebande muishond	
Helogale parvula	Dwarf Mongoose	Dwergmuishond	

ORDER TUBULIDENTATA

Family Orycteropodidae	Aardvarks		
Orycteropus afer	Aardvark	Erdvark	

ORDER PROBOSCIDEA

Family Elephantidae	Elephants		
Loxodonta africana	African Elephant	Afrika-olifant	

ORDER HYRACOIDEA

Family Procaviidae	Dassies		
Procavia capensis	Rock Dassie	Klipdas	

ORDER PERISSODACTYLA

Family Rhinocerotidae	Rhinoceros		
Ceratotherium simum	White Rhinoceros	Witrenoster	
Diceros bicornis	Black Rhinoceros	Swartrenoster	

Family Equidae	Zebra		
Equus quagga	Plains Zebra	Bontsebra	

ORDER CETARTIODACTYLA

| Family Suidae | Even-toed Ungulates | | |
	Pigs		
Potamochoerus larvatus	Bushpig	Bosvark	
Phacochoerus africanus	Warthog	Vlakvark	

ORDER RUMINANTIA

Family Giraffidae	Giraffes		
Giraffa camelopardalis	Giraffe	Kameelperd	

Family Bovidae	Antelopes and Buffalos		
Connochaetes taurinus	Blue Wildebeest	Blouwildebees	
Alcelaphus buselaphus	Red Hartebeest	Rooihartbees	
Damaliscus lunatus	Tsessebe	Tsessebe	
Sylvicapra grimmia	Common Duiker	Gewone Duiker	
Oreotragus oreotragus	Klipspringer	Klipspringer?	
Raphicerus campestris	Steenbok	Steenbok	
Aepyceros m. melampus	Impala	Rooibok	
Pelea capreolus	Grey Rhebok	Vaalribbok	RSA
Hippotragus equinus	Roan	Bastergemsbok	
Hippotragus niger	Sable	Swartwitpens	
Oryx gazella	Gemsbok	Gemsbok	
Syncerus caffer	Buffalo	Buffel	
Tragelaphus angasii	Nyala	Nyala	
Tragelaphus strepsiceros	Kudu	Koedoe	
Tragelaphus scriptus	Bushbuck	Bosbok	
Tragelaphus oryx	Eland	Eland	
Redunca arundinum	Reedbuck	Rietbok	
Redunca fulvorufula	Mountain Reedbuch	Rooiribbok	
Kobus ellipsiprymnus	Waterbuck	Waterbok	

Total: 124 species

Scientific and common names in brackets represent the former name of the birds before the name standardization revision of all bird species.

NON-PASSERINES

ORDER STRUTHIONIFORMES
Family Struthionidae   Ostriches
001   Struthio camelus   Common Ostrich

ORDER PODICIPEDIFORMES
Family Podicipedidae   Grebes
006   Podiceps cristatus   Great Crested Grebe
008   Tachybaptus ruficollis   Little Grebe (Dabchick)

ORDER PELECANIFORMES
Family Pelecanidae   Pelicans
050   Pelecanus rufescens   Pink-backed Pelican

ORDER PROCELLARIIFORMES
Family Phalacrocoracidae   Cormorants
055   Phalacrocorax [carbo] lucidus   White-breasted Cormorant
058   Phalacrocorax africanus   Reed (Long-tailed) Cormorant

Family Anhingidae   Darters
060   Anhinga rufa   African Darter

ORDER CICONIIFORMES
Family Ardeidae   Herons, Egrets and Bitterns
062   Ardea cinerea   Grey Heron
063   Ardea melanocephala   Black-headed Heron
064   Ardea goliath   Goliath Heron
065   Ardea purpurea   Purple Heron
066   Egretta alba   Great Egret (Great White Egret)
067   Egretta garzetta   Little Egret
068   Egretta intermedia   Yellow-billed Egret
069   Egretta ardesiaca   Black Egret
071   Bubulcus ibis   Cattle Egret
072   Ardeola ralloides   Squacco Heron
074   Butorides striatus   Green-backed Heron
076   Nycticorax nycticorax   Black-crowned Night-Heron
077   Gorsachius leuconotus   White-backed Night Heron
078   Ixobrychus minutus   Little Bittern
079   Ixobrychus sturmii (minutus)   Dwarf Bittern

Family Scopidae   Hamerkop
081   Scopus umbretta   Hamerkop

Family Ciconiidae   Storks
083   Ciconia ciconia   White Stork
084   Ciconia nigra   Black Stork
085   Ciconia abdimii   Abdim's Stork
089   Leptoptilos crumeniferus   Marabou Stork
090   Myctaria ibis   Yellow-billed Stork

Family Plataleidae   Ibises and Spoonbills
091   Threskiornis aethiopicus   African Sacred Ibis
093   Plegadis falcinellus   Glossy Ibis
094   Bostrychia hagedash   Hadeda Ibis
095   Platalea alba   African Spoonbill

ORDER PHOENICOPTERIFORMES
Family Phoenicopteridae   Flamingos
096   Phoenicopterus ruber   Greater Flamingo
097   Phoeniconaias minor   Lesser Flamingo

ORDER ANSERIFORMES
Family Anatidae   Ducks, Geese and Swans

099	Dendrocygna viduata	White-faced Duck
100	Dendrocygna bicolor	Fulvous Duck
101	Thalassornis leuconotus	White-backed Duck
102	Alopochen aegyptiacus	Egyptian Goose
103	Tadorna cana	South African Shelduck
104	Anas undulata	Yellow-billed Duck
105	Anas sparsa	African Black Duck
106	Anas capensis	Cape Teal
107	Anas hottentota	Hottentot Teal
108	Anas erythrorhyncha	Red-billed Teal
112	Anas smithii	Cape shoveller
113	Netta erythophthalma	Southern Pochard
114	Nettapus auritus	Pygmy Goose
115	Sarkidiornis melanotos	Comb (Knob-billed) Duck
116	Plectropterus gambensis	Spur-winged Goose
117	Oxyura maccoa	Maccoa Duck

ORDER FALCONIFORMES
Family Sagittariidae   Secretarybird

118	Sagittarius serpentarius	Secretarybird

Family Accipitridae   Vultures, Kites, Hawks, Eagles, Buzzards and Harriers

120	Neophron percnopterus	Egyptian Vulture
122	Gyps coprotheres	Cape Vulture
123	Gyps africanus	White-backed Vulture
124	Torgos tracheliotus	Lappet-faced Vulture
126a	Milvus migrans	Black Kite
126b	Milvus [m.] aegyptius (parasitus)	Yellow-billed Kite
127	Elanus caeruleus	Black-shouldered Kite
128	Aviceda cuculoides	African Cuckoo Hawk (African Baza)
130	Pernis apivorus	Honey Buzzard
131	Aquila verreauxii	Verreaux's (Black) Eagle
132	Aquila rapax	Tawny Eagle
133	Aquila nipalensis	Steppe Eagle
134	Aquila pomarina	Lesser Spotted Eagle
135	Aquila wahlbergi	Wahlberg's Eagle
136	Hieraaetus pennatus	Booted Eagle
137	Hieraaetus spilogaster	African Hawk-Eagle
138	Hieraaetus ayresii	Ayres' Eagle
139	Lophaetus occipitalis	Long-crested Eagle
140	Polemaetus bellicosus	Martial Eagle
142	Cicaetus cinereus	Brown Snake-Eagle
143	Circaetus pectoralis (gallicus)	Black-chested (-breasted) Snake Eagle
146	Terathopius ecaudatus	Bateleur
148	Haliaeetus vocifer	African Fish-Eagle
149	Buteo buteo	Common (Steppe) Buzzard
152	Buteo rufofuscus	Jackal Buzzard
154	Kaupifalco monogrammicus	Lizard Buzzard
156	Accipiter ovampensis	Ovambo Sparrowhawk
157	Accipiter minullus	Little Sparrowhawk
158	Accipiter melanoleucus	Black Sparrowhawk
159	Accipiter badius	Shikra (Little Banded Goshawk)
161	Melierax (Micronisus) gabar	Gabar Goshawk
162	Melierax canorus	Southern Pale Chanting Goshawk
165	Circus ranivorus	African Marsh Harrier
166	Circus pygargus	Montagu's Harrier
167	Circus macrourus	Pallid Harrier
169	Polyboroides typus	African Harrier-Hawk (Gymnogene)

Family Pandionidae   Ospreys

170	Pandion haliaetus	Osprey

Family Falconidae   Falcons and Kestrels

171	Falco peregrinus	Peregrine Falcon
172	Falco biarmicus	Lanner Falcon
173	Falco subbuteo	Hobby Falcon
179	Falco verspertinus	Western Red Footed Kestrel
180	Falco amurensis	Amur Falcon (Eastern Red-footed Kestrel)
181	Falco tinnunculus	Common (Rock) Kestrel

| 182 | Falco rupicoloides | | Greater Kestrel |
| 183 | Falco naumanni | | Lesser Kestrel |

ORDER GALLIFORMES
Family Phasianidae — Francolins and Quails

188	Peliperdix (Francolinus) coqui		Coqui Francolin
189	Peliperdix (Francolinus) sephaena		Crested Francolin
191	Scleroptila (Francolinus) shelleyi		Shelley's Francolin
196	Pternistes (Francolinus) natalensis		Natal Francolin
199	Pternistes (Francolinus) swainsonii		Swainson's Spurfowl (Swainson's Francolin)
200	Coturnix coturnix		Common Quail
201	Coturnix delegorguei		Harlequin Quail

Family Numididae — Guineafowls

| 203 | Numida meleagris | | Helmeted Guineafowl |

ORDER GRUIFORMES
Family Turnicidae — Buttonquails

| 205 | Turnix sylvatica | | Small (Kurrichane) Buttonquail |

Family Gruidae — Cranes

| 208 | Anthropoides paradisea | | Blue Crane |

Family Rallidae — Rails, Crakes, Flufftails, Gallinules, Moorhens and Coots

210	Rallus caerulescens		African Rail
212	Crex egregia		African Crake
213	Amaurornis flavirostris		Black Crake
215	Porzana pusilla		Baillon's Crake
217	Sarothrura rufa		Red-chested Flufftail
226	Gallinula chloropus		Common Moorhen
227	Gallinula angulata		Lesser Moorhen
228	Fulica cristata		Red-knobbed Coot

Family Otididae — Bustards and Korhaans

230	Ardeotis kori		Kori Bustard
231	Neotis denhami		Denham's (Stanley's) Bustard
233	Eupodites [s.] barrowii (cafra)		Barrow's (White-bellied) Korhaan
237	Eupodites ruficrista		Red-crested Korhaan
239b	Eupodites [afra] afraoides		Northern (White-winged) Korhaan

ORDER CHARADRIIFORMES
Family Jacanidae — Jacanas

| 240 | Actophilornis africanus | | African Jacana |

Family Rostratulidae — Painted Snipe

| 242 | Rostratula benghalensis | | Greater Painted-snipe (Painted Snipe) |

Family Charadriidae — Plovers

245	Charadrius haiticula		Ringed Plover
248	Charadrius pecuarius		Kittlitz's Plover
249	Charadrius tricollaris		Three-banded Plover
252	Charadrius asiaticus		Caspian Plover
255	Vanellus coronatus		Crowned Lapwing (Crowned Plover)
258	Vanellus armatus		Blacksmith Lapwing (Blacksmith Plover)
260	Vanellus senegallus		African Wattled Lapwing (Wattled Plover)

Family Scolopacidae — Turnstones, Sandpipers, Stints, Snipe and Curlews

264	Actitis (Tringa) hypoleucos		Common Sandpiper
265	Tringa ochropus		Green Sandpiper
266	Tringa glareola		Wood Sandpiper
268	Tringa totanus		Redshank
269	Tringa stagnatilis		Marsh Sandpiper
270	Tringa nebularia		Common Greenshank (Greenshank)
272	Calidris ferruginea		Curlew Sandpiper
274	Calidris minute		Little Stint
284	Philomachus pugnax		Ruff
286	Gallinago nigripennis		African (Ethiopian) Snipe

Family Recurvirostridae	Avocets and Stilts	
294 Recurvirostra avosetta		Avocet
295 Himantopus himantopus		Black-winged Stilt

Family Burhinidae	Dikkops	
297 Burhinus capensis		Spotted Thick-knee (Spotted Dikkop)
298 Burhinus vermiculatus		Water Thick-knee (Water Dikkop)

Family Glareolidae	Coursers and Pratincoles	
300 Cursorius temminckii		Temminck's Courser
303 Rhinoptilus chalcopterus		Bronze-winged (Violet-tipped) Courser
305 Glareola normanni		Black-winged Prantincole

SUB-ORDER LARI

Family Laridae	Skkuas, Gulls and Terns	
315 Larus cirrocephalus		Greyheaded Gull
338 Chlidonias hybrida		Whiskered Tern
339 Chlidonias leucopterus		Whitewinged Tern

ORDER PTEROCLIFORMES

Family Pteroclididae	Sandgrouse	
345 Pterocles burchelli		Burchell's Sandgrouse
346 Pterocles gutturalis		Yellow-throated Sandgrouse
347 Pterocles bicinctus		Double-banded Sandgrouse

ORDER COLUMBIFORMES

Family Columbidae	Pigeons and Doves	
348 Columba livia		Rock Dove (Feral Pigeon)
349 Columba guinea		Speckled (Rock) Pigeon
352 Streptopelia semitorquata		Red-eyed Dove
354 Streptopelia capicola		Cape Turtle-Dove
355 Streptopelia senegalensis		Laughing Dove
356 Oena capensis		Namaqua Dove
358 Turtur chalcospilos		Emerald-spotted Wood-Dove (Green-spotted Dove)
361 Treron calva		African Green-Pigeon

ORDER PSITTACIFORMES

Family Psittacidae	Parrots, Parakeets and Lovebirds	
364 Poicephalus meyeri		Meyer's Parrot

ORDER MUSOPHAGIFORMES

Family Musophagidae	Louries	
373 Corythaixoides concolor		Grey Go-away-bird (Grey Lourie)

ORDER Cuculiformes

Family Cuculidae	Cuckoos and Coucals	
374 Cuculus canorus		European Cuckoo
375 Cuculus gularis		African Cuckoo
377 Cuculus solitarius		Red-chested Cuckoo
378 Cuculus clamosus		Black Cuckoo
380 Clemator glandarius		Great Spotted Cuckoo
381 Oxylophus (Clemator) levaillantii		Levaillant's Cuckoo (African Striped Cuckoo)
382 Oxylophus (Clemator) jacobinus		Jacobin Cuckoo
385 Chrysococcyx klaas		Klaas's Cuckoo
386 Chrysococcyx caprius		Diderick Cuckoo
391a Centropus buchelli		Burchell's Coucal
391b Centropus superciliosus		White-browed Coucal

ORDER STRIGIFORMES

Family Tytonidae	Barn and Grass Owls	
392 Tyto alba		Barn Owl
393 Tyto capensis		African Grass Owl

Family Strigidae	Typical Owls	
395 Asio capensis		Marsh Owl
396 Otus senegalensis		African Scops Owl
397 Ptilopsus granti (Otus leucotis)		Southern White-faced Scops-Owl (White-faced Owl)
398 Glaucidium perlatum		Pearl-spotted Owlet

400	Bubo capensis		Cape Eagle-Owl
401	Bubo africanus		Spotted Eagle-Owl
402	Bubo lacteus		Verreaux's (Giant) Eagle-Owl

ORDER CAPRIMULGIFORMES
Family Caprimulgidae — Nightjars

404	Caprimulgus europaeus		European Nightjar
405	Caprimulgus pectoralis		Fiery-necked Nightjar
406	Caprimulgus rufigena		Rufous-cheeked Nightjar
408	Caprimulgus tristigma		Freckled Nightjar

ORDER APODIFORMES
Family Apodidae — Swifts

411	Apus apus		Common (European) Swift
412	Apus barbatus		African Black Swift
415	Apus caffer		White-rumped Swift
416	Apus horus		Horus Swift
417	Apus affinis		Little Swift
418	Apus melba		Alpine Swift
421	Cypsiurus parvus		African Palm Swift

ORDER COLIIFORMES
Family Coliidae — Mousebirds

424	Colius striatus		Speckled Mousebird
425	Colius colius		White-backed Mousebird
426	Colius indicus		Red-faced Mousebird

ORDER CARACIIFORMES
Family Halcyonidae — Kingfishers

428	Ceryle rudis		Pied Kingfisher
429	Megaceryle (Ceryle) maxima		Giant Kingfisher
430	Alcedo semitorquata		Half-collared Kingfisher
431	Alcedo cristata		Malachite Kingfisher
432	Ispidina picta		African Pygmy Kingfisher
433	Halcyon senegalensis		Woodland Kingfisher
435	Halcyon albiventris		Brown-hooded Kingfisher
436	Halcyon leucocephala		Grey-headed (-hooded) Kingfisher
437	Halcyon chelicuti		Striped Kingfisher

Family Meropidae — Bee-eaters

438	Merops apiaster		European Bee-eater
440	Merops persicus		Blue-cheeked Bee-eater
441	Merops nubicoides		Southern Carmine Bee-eater
443	Merops bullockoides		White-fronted Bee-eater
444	Merops pusillus		Little Bee-eater
445	Merops hirundineus		Swallow-tailed Bee-eater

Family Coraciidae — Rollers

446	Coracias garrulus		European Roller
447	Coracias caudatai		Lilac-breasted Roller
449	Coracias naevia		Purple Roller

Family Upupidae — Hoopoes

| 451 | Upupa africana | | African Hoopoe |

Family Phoeniculidae — Woodhoopoes

| 452 | Phoeniculus pupureus | | Green (Red-billed) Wood-Hoopoe |
| 454 | Rhinopomastus cyanomelas | | Common Scimitarbill (Scimitarbilled Wood-Hoopoe) |

Family Bucerotidae — Hornbills

457	Tockus nasutus		African Grey Hornbill
458	Tockus erythrorhynchus		Red-billed Hornbill
459	Tockus leucomelas (flavirostris)		Southern Yellow-billed Hornbill

ORDER PICIFORMES
Family Capitonidae — Barbets and Tinker Barbets

464	Lybius torquatus		Back-collared Barbet
465	Tricholaema leucomelas		African Pied Barbet
470	Pogoniulus chrysoconus		Yellow-fronted Tinker-bird (Yellow-front Tinker Barbet)
473	Trachyphonus vaillantii		Crested Barbet

Family Indicatoridae	Honeyguides	
474	Indicator indicator	Greater Honeyguide
476	Indicator minor	Lesser Honeyguide
478	Prodotiscus regulus	Sharpbilled Honeyguide

Family Picidae	Woodpeckers	
481	Campethera bennittii	Bennett's Woodpecker
483	Campethera abingoni	Golden-tailed Woodpecker
486	Dendropicos fuscescens	Cardinal Woodpecker
487	Dendropicos (Thripias) namaquus	Bearded Woodpecker

Family Jyngidae	Wrynecks	
489	Jynx ruficollis	Redthroated Wryneck

PASSERINES

ORDER PASSERIFORMES
SUBORDER PASSERES

Family Alaudidae	Larks	
493	Mirafra passerina	Monotonous Lark
494	Mirafra africana	Rufous-naped Lark
496	Mirafra rufocinnamomea	Flapped Lark
498	Mirafra sabota	Sabota Lark
505	Pinarocorys nigricans	Dusky Lark
507	Calandrella cinerea	Red-capped Lark
508	Spizocorys conirostris	Pink-billed Lark
515	Eremopterix leucotis	Chestnut-backed Sparrowlark (Finchlark)
516	Eremopterix verticalis	Grey-backed Sparrowlark (Finchlark)

Family Hirundinidae	Swallows and Martins	
518	Hirundo rustica	Barn (European) Swallow
520	Hirundo albigularis	White-throated Swallow
523	Hirundo dimidiata	Pearl-breasted Swallow
524	Hirundo semirufa	Red-breasted Swallow
526	Hirundo cucullata	Greater Striped Swallow
527	Hirundo abyssinica	Lesser Striped Swallow
528	Hirundo spilodera	South African Cliff Swallow
529	Hirundo fuligula	Rock Martin
530	Delichon urbica	Common House-Martin (House Martin)
532	Riparia riparia	Sand Martin
533	Riparia paludicola	Brown-throated Martin (Plain Martin)
534	Riparia cincta	Banded Martin

Family Campephagidae	Cukooshrike	
538	Campephaga flava	Back Cukooshrike

Family Dicruridae	Drongos	
541	Dicrurus adsimilis	Fork-tailed Drongo

Family Oriolidae	Orioles	
543	Oriolus oriolus	Eurasian (European) Golden Oriole
545	Oriolus larvatus	Black-headed Oriole

Family Corvidae	Crows and Ravens	
547	Corvus capensis	Black Crow
548	Corvus albus	Pied Crow

Family Paridae	Tits	
552	Parus cinerascens	Ashy Tit
554	Parus niger	Southern Black Tit

Family Ramizidae	Penduline Tits	
557	Anthoscopus minutus	Cape Penduline-Tit
558	Anthoscopus caroli	Grey Penduline-Tit

Family Timaliidae	Babblers	
560	Turdoides jardineii	Arrow-marked Babbler
563	Turdoides bicolor	Southern Pied Babbler

Family Pycnonotidae   Bulbuls

567	Pycnonotus nigricans	African Red-eyed Bulbul
568	Pycnonotus barbatus	Dark-capped (Black-eyed) Bulbul
569	Phyllastrephus terrestris	Terrestrial Brownbul (Terrestrial Bulbul)
574	Chlorocichla flaviventris	Yellow-bellied Greenbul (Yellow-bellied Bulbul)

Family Turdidae   Thrushes, Chats, Robins and Rockjumpers

576	Turdus libonyanus	Kurrichane Thrush
577	Turdus olivaceus	Olive Thrush
580	Psophocichla (Turdus) litsipsirupa	Groundscraper Thrush
581	Monticola rupestris	Cape Rock-Thrush
583	Monticola brevipes	Short-toed Rock-Thrush
586	Oenanthe monticola	Mountain Wheatear (Mountain Chat)
587	Oenanthe pileata	Capped Wheatear
588	Oenanthe bifasciata	Buff-streaked Chat
589	Cercomela familiaris	Familiar Chat
593	Thamnolaea cinnamomeiventris	Mocking Cliff-Chat (Mocking Chat)
595	Myrmecocichla formicivora	Anteating Chat
596	Saxicola torquata	African Stone Chat
601	Cossypha caffra	Cape Robin-Chat
602	Cossypha humeralis	White-throated Robin-Chat
609	Luscinia luscinia	Thrush Nightingale
613	Cossypha (Erythropygia) leucophrys	White-browed Scrub-Robin (White-browed Robin)
615	Cercotrichas (Erythropygia) paena	Kalahari Scrub-Robin (Kalahari Robin)

Family Sylviidae   Warblers, Apalises, Crombecs, Eremomelas, Cisticolas and Prinias

619	Sylvia borin	Garden Warbler
620	Sylvia communis	Whitethroat
621	Parisoma subcaeruleum	Chestnut-vented Tit-babbler (Titbabbler)
625	Hippolais icterina	Icterine Warbler
626	Hippolais olivetorum	Olive-tree Warbler
628	Acrocephalus arundinadeus	Great Reed-Warbler
631	Acrocephalus baeticatus	African Reed-Warbler (African March Warbler)
633	Acrocephalus palustris	European Marsh Warbler
634	Acrocephalus schoenobaenus	European Sedge Warbler
635	Acrocephalus gracilirostris	Lesser Swamp-Warbler (Cape Reed Warbler)
638	Bradypterus baboecala	African Sedge Warbler
643	Phylloscopus trochilus	Willow Warbler
645	Apalis thoracica	Bar-throated Apalis
651	Sylvietta rufescens	Long-billed Crombec
653	Eremomela icteropygialis	Yellow-bellied Eremomela
656	Eremomela usticollis	Burnt-necked Eremomela
657b	Camaroptera brevicaudata	Grey-backed Camaroptera (Bleating Warbler)
658	Calamonastes (Camaroptera) fasciolatus	Barred Wren-Warbler (African Barred Warbler)
661	Sphenoeacus afer	Cape Grassbird
664	Cisticola juncidis	Zitting (Fantailed) Cisticola
665	Cisticola aridulus	Desert Cisticola
667	Cisticola ayresii	Ayres' Cisticola
671	Cisticola rufilata	Tinkling Cisticola
672	Cisticola chinianus	Rattling Cisticola
677	Cisticola tinniens	Levaillant's Cisticola
679	Cisticola aberrans	Lazy Cisticola
681	Cisticola fulvicapillus	Neddicky (Piping Cisticola)
683	Prinia subflava	Tawny-flanked Prinia
685	Prinia flavicans	Black-chested Prinia

Family Muscicapidae   Flycatchers and Batises

689	Muscicapa striata	Spotted Flycatcher
693	Myioparus plumbeus	Grey Tit-Flycatcher (Fan-tailed Flycatcher)
694	Melaenornis pammelaina	Southern Black Flycatcher
695	Bradornis (Melaenornis) mariquensis	Marico Flycatcher
696	Melaenornis pallidis	Pale (Pallid) Flycatcher (Mouse-coloured Flycatcher)
698	Sigelus silens	Fiscal Flycatcher
701	Batis molitor	Chinspot Batis
706	Stenostira scita	Fairy Flycatcher
710	Terpsiphone viridis	African Paradise-Flycatcher

Family Motacillidae	Wagtails, Pipits and Longclaws	
711	Motacilla aguimp	African Pied Wagtail
713	Motacilla capensis	Cape Wagtail
714	Motacilla flava	Yellow Wagtail
716	Anthus cinnamomeus	African (Grassveld) Pipit
717	Anthus similis	Long-billed Pipit
718	Anthus leucophrys	Plain-backed Pipit
719	Anthus vaalensis	Buffy Pipit
720	Anthus lineiventris	Striped Pipit
722	Anthus rivialis	Tree Pipit
723	Anthus caffer	Bushveld Pipit (Bush Pipit)
727	Macronyx capensis	Cape (Orange-throated) Longclaw

Family Laniidae	Shrikes	
731	Lanius minor	Lesser Grey Shrike
732	Lanius collaris	Common Fiscal (Fiscal Shrike)
733	Lanius collurio	Red-backed Shrike
735	Convinella melanoleuca	Magpie (Long-tailed) Shrike

Family Malaconotidae	Boubous, Tchagras and Bush Shrikes	
736	Laniarius ferrugineus	Southern Boubou
739	Laniarius atrococcineus	Crimson-breasted Shrike
740	Dryoscopus cubla	Black-backed Puffback (Puffback)
741	Nilaus afer	Brubru
743	Tchagra australis	Brown-crowned (Three-streaked) Tchagra
744	Tchagra senegala	Black-crowned Tchagra
748	Telophorus sulfureopectus	Orange-breasted Bush-Shrike
751	Malaconotus blanchoti	Grey-headed Bush-Shrike

Family Prionopidae	Helmetshrikes	
753	Prionops plumatus	White-creasted Helmet-Shrike (White Helmetshrike)
756	Eurocephalus anguitimens	Southern White-crowned Shrike

Family Sturnidae	Starlings and Mynas	
760	Creatophora cinerea	Wattled Starling
761	Cinnyricinclus leucogaster	Violet-backed (Plum-coloured) Starling
762	Lamprotornis australis	Burchell's Starling
764	Lamprotornis nitens	Cape Glossy Starling
765	Lamprotornis chalybaeus	Greater Blue-eared Starling
769	Onychognathus morio	Red-winged Starling

Family Buphagidae	Oxpeckers	
772	Buphagus erythrorhynchus	Red-billed Oxpecker

Family Promeropidae	Sugarbirds	
774	Promerops gurneyi	Gurney's Sugarbird

Family Nectariniidae	Sunbirds	
775	Nectarinia famosa	Malachite Sunbird
779	Cinnyris (Nectarinia) mariquensis	Marico Sunbird
785	Cinnyris (Nectarinia) afria	Greater Double-collared Sunbird
787	Cinnyris (Nectarinia) talatala	White-bellied Sunbird
792	Chalcomitra (Nectarinia) amethystina	Amethyst (Black) Sunbird

Family Zosteropidae	White-eyes	
796	Zosterops pallidus	Cape White-eye

Family Ploceidae	Sparrows, Weavers, Bishops, Widows and Queleas	
798	Bubalornis niger	Red-billed Buffalo-Weaver
799	Plocepasser mahali	White-browed Sparrow-Weaver
801	Passer domesticus	House Sparrow
802	Passer motitensis	Great Sparrow
803	Passer melanurus	Cape Sparrow
804	Passer diffusus (griseus)	Southern Grey-headed Sparrow
805	Petronia superciliaris	Yellow-throated Petronia (Yellow-throated Sparrow)
806	Scoropipes squamifrons	Scaly-feathered Finch
811	Ploceus cucullatus	Village (Spotted-backed) Weaver
813	Ploceus capensis	Cape Weaver

814	Ploceus velatus	Southern Masked-Weaver
815	Ploceus intermedius	Lesser Masked-Weaver
819	Anaplectus rubriceps	Red-headed Weaver
820	Anomalospiza imberbis	Cuckoo Finch
821	Quelea quelea	Red-billed Quelea
824	Euplectes orix	Southern Red Bishop
826	Euplectes afer	Yellow-crowned (Golden) Bishop
829	Euplectes albanotatus	White-winged Widow
831	Euplectes ardens	Red-collared Widow
832	Euplectes progne	Long-tailed Widow

Family Estildidae — Twinspots, Firefinches, Waxbills and Mannikins

834	Pytilia melba	Green-winged Pytilia (Melba Finch)
840	Lagonosticta rubricata	African (Blue-billed) Firefinch
841	Lagonosticta rhodopareia	Jameson's Firefinch
842	Lagonosticta senegala	Red-billed Firefinch
844	Uraeginthus angolensis	Blue Waxbill (Blue-breasted Cordonbleu)
845	Granatina (Uraeginthus) granatinus	Violet-eared Waxbill (Common Grenadier)
846	Estrilda astrild	Common Waxbill
847	Estrilda erythronotos	Black-faced (Black-cheeked) Waxbill
850	Estrilda melanotis	Swee Waxbill
852	Ortygospiza atricollis	African Quailfinch
854	Amandava (Sporaeginthus) subflava	Orange-breasted Waxbill (Zebra Waxbill)
855	Amadina fasciata	Cut-throat Finch
856	Amadina erythrocephala	Red-headed Finch
857	Lonchura (Spermester) cucullata	Bronze Mannikin

Family Viduidae — Whydahs and Widowfinches

860	Vidua macroura	Pin-tailed Whydah
861	Vidua regia	Shaft-tailed Whydah
862	Vidua paradisaea	Long-tailed Paradise-Whydah (Paradise Whydah)
864	Vidua funerea	Dusky Indigobird (Black Widow-finch)
865	Vidua purpurascens	Pruple Indigobird (Purple Widow-finch)
867	Vidua chalybeata	Village Indigobird (Steelblue Widow-finch)

Family Fringillidae — Canaries and Buntings

869	Serinus mozambicus	Yellow-fronted (Yellow-eyed) Canary
870	Serinus atrogularis	Black-throated Canary
873	Serinus scotops	Forest Canary (Unconfirmed)
878	Serinus flaviventris	Yellow Canary
881	Serinus gularis	Streaky-headed Seedeater (Streaky-headed Canary)
884	Emberiza flaviventris	Golden-breasted Bunting
885	Emberiza capensis	Cape Bunting
886	Emberiza tahapisi	Cinnamon-breasted (Rock) Bunting
887	Emberiza impetuani	Larklike Bunting

Total: 412 species

| CLASS: | REPTILIA | REPTILES |
| ORDER: | SQUAMATA | SCALE-BEARING REPTILES |

SUBORDER: LACERTILIA — LIZARDS

Family Gekkonidae — Geckos
Homopholis wahlbergi	Wahlberg's Velvet Gecko
Hemidactylus mabouia	Tropical House Gecko
Lygodactylus capensis capensis #	Cape Dwarf Gecko
Lygodactylus waterbergensis	Waterberg Dwarf Gecko
Pachydactylus affinis #	Transvaal Thick-toed Gecko
Pachydactylus turneri #	Turner's Thick-toed Gecko

Family Agamidae — Agamas
Acanthocercus atricollis #	Tree Agama
Agama aculeata distanti #	Distant's Ground Agama

Family Chamaeleonidae — Chameleons
Chamaeleo dilepis #	Flap-necked Chameleon

Family Scincidae — Skinks
Scelotes limpopoensis limpopoensis	Limpopo Dwarf Burrowing Skink
Mabuya margaritifer	Five-lined or Rainbow Skink
Mabuya capensis	Cape Skink
Mabuya varia #	Variable Skink
Mabuya punctatissima #	Speckled Skink
Lygosoma sundevallii	Sundevall's Writhing Skink
Panaspis wahlbergii	Wahlberg's Snake-eyed Skink
Acontias percivali occidentalis	Percival's Legless Skink

Family Lacertidae — Old World Lizards or Lacertids
Nucras intertexta	Spotted Sandveld Lizard
Heliobolus lugubris	Bushveld Lizard
Pedioplanis lineoocellata pulchella	Spotted Sand Lizard
Ichnotropis capensis	Cape Rough-scaled Lizard

Family: Varanidae — Monitors
Varanus albigularis	White-throated Monitor
Varanus niloticus	Nile or Water Monitor

Family Gerrhosauridae — Plated Lizards
Gerrhosaurus validus	Giant Plated Lizard
Gerrhosaurus flavigularis #	Yellow-throated Plated lizard

Family Cordylidae — Girdle-tailed Lizard
Cordylus breyeri	Waterberg Girdled Lizard
Cordylus jonesi #	Jones' Girdled Lizard
Cordylus vittifer	Transvaal Girdled Lizard
Cordylus (Pseudocordylus) transvaalensis	Northern Crag Lizard
Platysaurus guttatus	Dwarf Flat Lizard
Platysaurus minor	Waterberg Flat Lizard

SUBORDER: AMPHISBAENIA — AMPHISBENIDS or WORM LIZARDS

Family Amphisbaenidae — Tropical Worm Lizards
Zygaspis quadrifrons	Kalahari Round-headed Worm Lizard

SUBORDER: SERPENTES — SNAKES

Family Typhlopidae — Blind Snakes
Rhinotyphlops lalandei #	Delalande's Beaked Blind Snake

Family Leptotyphlopidae — Thread Snakes
Leptotyphlops incognitus	Eastern Thread Snake
Leptotyphlops scutifrons	Peters' Thread Snake
Leptotyphlops distanti	Distant's Thread Snake

Family Pythonidae   Pythons
Python natalensis #   Southern Rock Python

Family Atractaspididae   African Burrowing Snakes
Atractaspis bibronii   Bibron's Side-stabbing Snake
Aparallactus capensis #   Cape Centipede-eater
Amblyodipsas polylepis   Common Purple-glossed Snake

Family Colubridae   Typical Snakes
Lamprophis fuliginosus   Brown House Snake
Lycophidion capense capense #   Cape Wolf Snake
Mehelya capensis capensis #   Cape File Snake
Mehelya nyassae   Black File Snake
Pseudaspis cana #   Mole Snake
Psammophis jallae   Jalla's Sand Snake
Psammophis subtaeniatus subtaeniatus #   Stripe-bellied Sand Snake
Psammophis brevirostris brevirostris   Short-snouted Sand Snake
Psammophis angolensis   Dwarf Sand Snake
Philothamnus hoplogaster   Green Water Snake
Philothamnus semivariegatus #   Spotted Bush Snake
Crotaphopeltis hotamboeia #   Herald or Red-lipped Snake
Telescopus semiannulatus semiannnulatus #   Eastern Tiger Snake
Dispholidus typus typus #   Boomslang
Thelotornis capensis capensis #   Twig Snake
Dasypeltis scabra   Common or Rhombic Egg-eater

Family Elapidae   Cobras, Mambas and others
Elapsoidea boulengeri   Boulenger's Garter Snake
Naja annulifera annulifera #   Snouted Cobra
Naja mossambica #   Mozambique Spitting Cobra
Dendroaspis polylepis #   Black Mamba

Family Viperidae   Adders
Causus defilippii #   Snouted Night Adder
Bitis caudalis   Horned Adder
Bitis arietans arietans #   Puff Adder

ORDER: TESTUDINES   TORTOISES

SUBORDER: CRYPTODIRA   Modern Tortoises

Family Testudinidae   Land Tortoises
Geochelone pardalis #   Leopard Tortoise
Psammobates oculiferus   Serrated or Kalahari Tent Tortoise
Kinixys lobatsiana #   Lobatse Hinged Tortoise

SUBORDER: PLEURODIRA   Side-necked Terrapins

Family Pelomedusidae   Side-necked Terrapins
Pelomedusa subrufa   Marsh or Helmeted Terrapin
Pelusios sinuatus   Serrated Hinged Terrapin

| CLASS: | AMPHIBIA | AMPHIBIANS |
| ORDER: | ANURA | FROGS |

Family Pipidae   Clawed Frogs
Xenopus laevis laevis #   Common Platanna

Family Bufonidae   Toads
Bufo gutturalis #   Guttural Toad
Bufo maculatus   Flat-backed Toad
Bufo poweri #   Power's Toad
Bufo fenhoulheti fenhoulheti   Northern Pigmy Toad
Schismaderma carens #   Red Toad

Family Microhylidae   Rain Frogs
Breviceps adspersus   Bushveld Rain Frog
Phrynomantis bifasciatus #   Banded Rubber Frog

Family Ranidae   Common Frogs
Pyxicephalus edulis   Edible Bullfrog
Tomopterna cryptotis #   Tremolo Sand Frog
(Tomopterna krugerensis?)   Knocking Sand Frog
Tomopterna natalensis #   Natal Sand Frog
Afrana angolensis #   Common River Frog
Strongylopus fasciatus   Striped Stream Frog
Ptychadena anchietae   Anchieta's Ridged Frog
Ptychadena porosissima   Grassland Ridged Frog
Phrynobatrachus natalensis #   Natal Puddle Frog

Family Rhacophoridae   Foam Nest Frogs
Chiromantis xerampelina #   Grey Tree Frog

Family Hyperoliidae   Reed Frogs
Kassina senegalensis   Senegal Kassina

The above list of species was compiled from records from the quarter degree squares (qds) which cover the area of the park or those immediately next to them, which makes it likely that several of these will still be recorded from within the park limits in future. Those species marked # were confirmed by staff on site. A number of the yet unconfirmed species may not actually occur within the park limits due to the absence of suitable habitat.

SPIDERS OF MARAKELE NATIONAL PARK

PPRI NUMBER	FAMILY	GENUS	SPECIES
AcAT 91/1172	Araneidae	Argiope	A. australis
AcAT 91/219	Araneidae	Argiope	A. australis
AcAT 89/346	Araneidae	Cyclosa	
AcAT 91/270	Araneidae	Cyclosa	
AcAT 91/586	Araneidae	Cyrtophora	C. citricola
AcAT 91/268	Araneidae		
AcAT 76/1876	Araneidae	Pararaneus	P. spectator
AcAT 80/121	Ctenidae	NONE	
Literature	Gnaphosidae	Asemesthes	montanus
	Hersiliidae	Hersilia	
AcAT 91/262	Lycosidae	Evippomma	
AcAT 91/267	Lycosidae	NONE	
AcAT 91/277	Lycosidae	NONE	
AcAT 91/587	Miturgidae	Cheiracanthium	C. furculatum
AcAT 91/269	Oxyopidae		
AcAT 91/274	Oxyopidae		
AcAT 89/367	Oxyopidae	Oxyopes	
AcAT 86/550	Oxyopidae	Oxyopes	
AcAT 91/265	Oxyopidae	Oxyopes	
AcAT 91/264	Oxyopidae	Oxyopes	
AcAT 91/272	Pholcidae	Smeringopus	S. natalensis
	Pisauridae	Euprosthenops	
	Selenopidae	Anyphops	
AcAT 83/215	Sicariidae	Loxosceles	
AcAT 80/174	Sparassidae	Eusparassus	
AcAT 89/371	Sparassidae	Olios	
AcAT 91/189	Tetragnathidae	Nephila	N. senegalensis annulata
AcAT 81/222	Theraphosidae	Brachionopus	
AcAT 81/656	Theraphosidae	Ceratogyrus	C. bechuanicus
AcAT 80/113	Theraphosidae	Ceratogyrus	C. bechuanicus
AcAT 80/115	Theraphosidae	Ceratogyrus	C. bechuanicus
AcAT 80/145	Theraphosidae	Ceratogyrus	C. bechuanicus
AcAT 97/793	Theraphosidae	Ceratogyrus	C. bechuanicus
AcAT 83/243	Theraphosidae	Harpactirella	
AcAT 91/273	Theraphosidae	NONE	
AcAT 91/95	Theraphosidae	Pterinochilus	
AcAT 91/503	Theraphosidae	Pterinochilus	
AcAT 81/316	Theridiidae	Episinus	
AcAT 82/756	Thomisidae	Camaricus	
AcAT 88/484	Thomisidae	Camaricus	
AcAT 2000/439	Thomisidae	Diaea	D. punctata
AcAT 81/62	Thomisidae	Monaeses	M. austrinus
AcAT 80/69	Thomisidae	Monaeses	M. paradoxus
AcAT 80/70	Thomisidae	Runcinia	R. flavida
AcAT 80/67	Thomisidae	Runcinia	R. flavida
AcAT 91/588	Thomisidae	Runcinia	R. flavida
AcAT 91/278	Thomisidae	Runcinia	R. flavida
AcAT 86/861	Thomisidae	Synema	
AcAT 86/561	Thomisidae	Synema	
AcAT 79/354	Thomisidae	Thomisus	T. granulatus
AcAT 79/353	Thomisidae	Thomisus	T. scrupeus
AcAT 90/160	Thomisidae	Xysticus	
AcAT 89/357	Uloboridae	Uloborus	U. plumipes
AcAT 91/259	Zodariidae	Capheris	
AcAT 91/266	Zodariidae	Cydrela	

The information on this list was drawn from the database of the National Collection of Arachnida, Plant Protection Research Institute, Agricultural Research Council, Pretoria

PROVINCE	MAJOR LOCALITY	MINOR LOCALITY	LATITUDE	LONGITUDE
.Limpopo..	Thabazimbi		24.36S	27.24E
.Limpopo..	Thabazimbi		24.36S	27.24E
.Limpopo..	Thabazimbi	Shabalala	24.36S	27.24E
.Limpopo..	Thabazimbi		24.36S	27.24E
.Limpopo..	Thabazimbi		24.36S	27.24E
.Limpopo..	Thabazimbi	Koedoeskop	24.36S	27.24E
.Limpopo..	Thabazimbi		24.36S	27.24E
.Limpopo..	Thabazimbi	Farm 'Elandsfontein', Buffelshoek	24.36S	27.24E
Limpopo	Waterberg mt			
Limpopo	Thabazimbi			
.Limpopo..	Thabazimbi	Koedoeskop	24.36S	27.24E
.Limpopo..	Thabazimbi	Koedoeskop	24.36S	27.24E
.Limpopo..	Thabazimbi	Koedoeskop	24.36S	27.24E
.Limpopo..	Thabazimbi		24.36S	27.24E
.Limpopo..	Thabazimbi	Koedoeskop	24.36S	27.24E
.Limpopo..	Thabazimbi	Koedoeskop	24.36S	27.24E
.Limpopo..	Thabazimbi	Shabalala	24.36S	27.24E
.Limpopo..	Thabazimbi	Kransberg	24.36S	27.24E
.Limpopo..	Thabazimbi	Koedoeskop	24.36S	27.24E
.Limpopo..	Thabazimbi	Koedoeskop	24.36S	27.24E
.Limpopo..	Thabazimbi	Koedoeskop	24.36S	27.24E
.Limpopo..	Thabazimbi			
.Limpopo..	Thabazimbi			
.Limpopo..	Thabazimbi	37 km W of Thabazimbi	24.36S	27.24E
.Limpopo..	Thabazimbi	Farm Elandsfontein', 37 km W	24.36S	27.24E
.Limpopo..	Thabazimbi	Shabalala	24.36S	27.24E
.Limpopo..	Thabazimbi		24.36S	27.24E
.Limpopo..	Thabazimbi		24.36S	27.24E
.Limpopo..	Thabazimbi	Farm 'Elandsfontein'	24.36S	27.24E
.Limpopo..	Thabazimbi	Farms 'Elandsfontein', Buffelshoek, 37 km W	24.36S	27.24E
.Limpopo..	Thabazimbi	Farms 'Elandsfontein', Buffelshoek, 37 km W	24.36S	27.24E
.Limpopo..	Thabazimbi	Farms 'ElandSfontein', Buffelshoek, 37 km W	24.36S	27.24E
.Limpopo..	Thabazimbi	Farm 'Elandsfontein', Buffelshoek	24.36S	27.24E
.Limpopo..	Thabazimbi	Buffelshoek, 37 km W	24.24S	27.24E
.Limpopo..	Thabazimbi	Koedoeskop	24.36S	27.24E
.Limpopo..	Thabazimbi	Kransberg	24.36S	27.24E
.Limpopo..	Thabazimbi		24.36S	27.24E
.Limpopo..	Thabazimbi	Farm 'Elandsfontein'	24.36S	27.24E
.Limpopo..	Thabazimbi	Farm 'Elandsfontein'	24.36S	27.24E
.Limpopo..	Thabazimbi	Elandfontein	24.36S	27.24E
.Limpopo..	Palala river	Waterberg	2305S	27.53E
.Limpopo..	Thabazimbi		24.36S	27.24E
.Limpopo..	Thabazimbi	Farm 'Elandsfontein', 37 km W	24.36S	27.24E
.Limpopo..	Thabazimbi	Farm 'Elandsfontein', 37 km W	24.36S	27.24E
.Limpopo..	Thabazimbi	Farm 'Elandsfontein'	24.36S	27.24E
.Limpopo..	Thabazimbi		24.36S	27.24E
.Limpopo..	Thabazimbi	Koedoeskop	24.36S	27.24E
.Limpopo..	Thabazimbi	Kransberg	24.36S	27.24E
.Limpopo..	Thabazimbi	Kransberg	24.36S	27.24E
.Limpopo..	Thabazimbi		24.36S	27.24E
.Limpopo..	Thabazimbi		24.36S	27.24E
.Limpopo..	Thabazimbi	Kransberg	24.36S	27.24E
.Limpopo..	Thabazimbi	Shabalala	24.36S	27.24E
.Limpopo..	Koedoeskop	Thabazimbi	24.52S	27.31E
.Limpopo..	Koedoeskop	Thabazimbi	24.52S	27.31E

The plant species in the study area were identified through the H.G.W.J. Schweikerdt Herbarium at the University of Pretoria and the National Herbarium in Pretoria. The 966 plant species were classified in 151 families and 502 genera. The Bryophyta consist of 18 families, 26 genera and 46 species. The Pteridophyta consist of 12 families, 18 genera and 26 species. The Gymnospermae consist of three families, three genera and three species. The monocotyledonae consist of 21 families, 127 genera and 268 species. The dicotyledonae consist of 97 families, 331 genera and 649 species. The plant families and genera were classified according to Arnold & De Wet (1993). Species are listed alphabetically within each genus.

1. Schweikerdt Herbarium, University of Pretoria
2. National Herbarium, Botanical Research Institute, Private Bag X101 Pretoria 0001

BRYOPHYTA

RICCIACEAE
0001016	Riccia L.	
500	R. atropurpurea Sim	
1050	R. congoana Steph.	
1875	R. microciliata Volk & Perold	
1890	R. moenkemeyeri Steph.	
2100	R. okahanjana S. Arnell.	
3200	R. stricta (Lindenb.) Perold.	
3400	R. volkii S.W. Arnell.	

TARCHIONIACEAE
0001022 Targionia L.
100   T. hypophylla L.

AYTONIACEAE
0001036 Asterella Beauv.
200   A. bachmannii (Steph.) S.W. Arnell.
400   A. muscicola (Steph.) S.W. Arnell.
500   A. wilmsii (Steph.) S.W. Arnell.
0001038 Plagiochasma Lehm. & Lindenb.
150   P. appendiculatum Lehm. & Lindenb.
250   P. beccarianum Steph.
600   P. microcephalum (Steph.) Steph.
700   P. rupestre (Forst.) Steph. var. volkii Bischl.

EXORMOTHECACEAE
0001046 Exormotheca Mitt.
100   E. holstii Steph.
300   E. pastulosa Mitt.

CODONIACEAE
0001051 Fossombronia Roddi
200   F. crispa Nees.

SPHAGNACEAE
0001301 Sphagnum L.
200   S. capense Hornsch.
600   S. violascens C. Mull.

FISSIDENTACEAE
0001316 Fissidens Hedw.
750   F. bryoides Hedw.
4100   F. rufescens Horsch.
4500   F. submarginatus Bruch ex Krauss.

DITRICHACEAE
0001331 Ceratodon Brid.
100   C. purpureus (Hedw.) Brid. subsp. stenocarpus (B.S.G.) Dix.

DICRANACEAE
0001359 Campylopus Brid.
200   C. savannarum (C. Mull.) Mitt.
0001368 Trematodon Michx.
400   T. intermedius Welw. & Duby.

POTTIACEAE
0001426 Trichostomum Bruch
100   T. brachydontium Bruch ex F. A. Mull.
0001429 Weissia Hedw.
100   W. controvesa Hedw.

GIGASPERMACEAE
0001448 Oedipodiella Dix.
100   O. australis (Wag. & Dix.) Dix.

FUNARIACEAE
0001467 Funaria Hedw.
350   F. rottleri (Schwagr.) Broth.

BRYACEAE
0001507 Brachymenium Schwaegr.
100   B. acuminatum Harv. in Hook.
0001508 Bryum Hedw.
200   B. argenteum Hedw.
900   B. capillare Hedw.
1850   B. pycnophyllum (Dixon) Mohamed. B. sp.
0001512 Mielichloferia Nees & Hornsch.
100   M. bryoides (Harv.) Wijk & Marg.
0001515 Pohlia Hedw.
50   P. baronii Wijk & Marg.

BARTRAMIACEAE
0001584 Philonotis Brid.
100   P. africana (C. Mull.) Paris
550   P. falcata (Hook) Mitt.

PTYCHOMITRIACEAE
0001612 Ptychomitrium Fuernr.
200   P. crispatum (Hedw.) Jaeg.

LEUCODONTACEAE
0001687 Leucodon Schwaegr.
50   L. assimilis (C. Mull.) Jaeg.

METEORIACEAE
0001744 Pilotrichella (C. Mull.) Besch.
100   P. panduraefolia (C. Mull.) Jaeg.

POLYTRICHACEAE
0001921 Atrichum P. Beauv.
100   A. androgynum (C. Mull.) Jaeg.
0001922 Pogonathum P. Beauv.
100   P. capense (Hampe) Jaeg.
0001923 Polytrichum Hedw.
100   P. commune Hedw.

PTERIDOPHYTA

LYCOPODIACEAE
0000020 Lycopodium L.
300   L. cernuum L.

SELAGINELLACEAE
0000030 Selaginella Beauv.
100   S. caffrorum (Milde) Hieron.
200   S. dregei (Presl) Hieron.

OSMUNDACEAE
0000080 Osmunda L.
100   O. regalis L.

SCHIZAEACEAE
0000100 Anemia Swartz
200   A. simii Tardieu
0000120 Mohria Swartz
100   M. caffrorum (L.) Desv. var. caffrorum

HYMENOPHYLLACEAE
0000170 Trichomanes L.
500   T. rigidum Swartz

CYATHEACEAE
0000180 Cyathea J.E. Sm.
200   C. dregei Kunze

DENNSTAEDTIACEAE
0000260 Pteridium Gled ex Scop.
100   P. aquilinum (L.) Kuhn

ADIANTACEAE
0000290 Actiniopteris Link
200   A. radiata (Koenig ex Swartz) Link
0000340 Cheilanthes Swartz
770   C. hirta Sw. var. brevipilosa W. & N. Jacobsen
800   C. hirta Swartz var. hirta
1250   C. multifida (Sw.) Sw. subsp. lacerata N.C. Anthony & Schelpe
1400   C. parviloba (Swartz) Swartz
1900   C. viridis (Forssk.) Swartz var. viridis
0000360 Pellaea Link
200   P. calomelanos (Swartz) Link var. calomelanos
0000380 Pteris L.
300   P. cretica L.

POLYPODIACEAE
0000450 Pleopeltis H.B.K. ex Willd
100   P. excavata (Bory ex Willd.) Sledge.
400   P. schraderi (Mett.) Tardieu.

ASPLENIACEAE
0000520 Asplenium L.
300   A. aethiopicum (Burm. f.)
        Becherer
600   A. boltonii Hook. ex Schelpe
2900   A. splendens Kunze
0000530 Ceterach DC.
100   C. cordatum (Thunb.) Desv.

DRYOPTERIDACEAE
0000620 Dryopteris Adans.
300   D. inaequilis (Schltdl.) Kuntze
0000680 Woodsia R. Br.
50   W. angolensis Schelpe.

BLECHNACEAE
0000690 Blechnum L.
100   B. attenuatum (Swartz) Mett.
        var. giganteum (Kaulf.) Bonap.

GYMNOSPERMAE

ZAMIACEAE
0005000 Encephalartos Lehm.
600   E. eugene-maraisii Verdoorn
        subsp. eugene-maraisii

PODOCARPACEAE
0013000 Podocarpus L'Hérit. ex Pers.
400   P. latifolius (Thunb.) R. Br. Ex
        Mirb.

CUPRESSACEAE
0038010 Widdringtonia Endl.
200   W. nodiflora (L.) Powrie

ANGIOSPERMAE

MONOCOTYLEDONAE

TYPHACEAE
0049000 Typha L.
20   T. capensis (Rohrb.) N.E. Br.

POACEAE
9900100 Ischaemum L.
200   I. fasciculatum Brongn.
9900170 Urelytrum Hack.
100   U. agropyroides (Hack.) Hack.
9900280 Elionurus Kunth ex Willd.
100   E. muticus (Spreng.) Kunth
9900370 Imperata Cirillo
50   I. cylindrica (L.) Raeuschel
9900380 Miscanthus Anderss.
500   M. junceus (Stapf.) Pilg.
9900460 Sorghum Moench.
3700   S. versicolor Anderss.
9900500 Chrysopogon Trin.
200   C. serrulatus Trin.
9900630 Bothriochloa Kuntze
150   B. insculpta (A. Rich.)
        A. Camus
500   B. radicans (Lehm.) A. Camus
9900680 Schizachyrium Nees
400   S. sanguineum (Retz.) Alst.
9900710 Andropogon L.
200   A. appendiculatus Nees
350   A. chinensis (Nees) Merr.
500   A. eucomus Nees
900   A. huillensis Rendle

1600   A. schirensis A. Rich.
9900720 Cymbopogon Spreng.
200   C. excavatus (Hochst.) Stapf
        ex Burtt Davy
400   C. plurinodis (Stapf) Stapf ex
        Burtt Davy
600   C. validus (Stapf.) Stapf ex
        Burtt Davy
9900730 Hyparrhenia Fourn.
100   H. anamesa Clayton
1000   H. hirta (L.) Stapf
1200   H. newtonii (Hack.) Stapf var.
        newtonii
9900731 Hyperthelia Clayton
100   H. dissoluta (Nees ex Steud.)
        Clayton
9900750 Monocymbium Stapf
100   M. ceresiiforme (Nees) Stapf
9900780 Trachypogon Nees
100   T. spicatus (L. f.) Kuntze
9900800 Heteropogon Pers.
100   H. contortus (L.) Roem. &
        Schult.
300   H. melanocarpus (Elliott)
        Benth.
9900810 Diheteropogon (Hack.) Stapf
100   D. amplectens (Nees) Clayton
9900830 Themeda Forssk.
100   T. triandra Forssk.
9900890 Digitaria Haller
600   D. brazzae (Franch.) Stapf
1000   D. diagonalis (Nees) Stapf
        var. diagonalis
1400   D. eriantha Steud.
2700   D. monodactyla (Nees) Stapf
4400   D. tricholaenoides Stapf
9900940 Alloteropsis Presl.
250   A. semialata (R. Br.) Hitch.
        subsp. semialata
9901040 Brachiaria (Trin.) Griseb.
250   B. bovonei (Chiov.) Robyns
300   B. brizantha (A. Rich.) Stapf
1300   B. nigropedata (Fical. & Hiern)
        Stapf
1700   B. serrata (Thunb.) Stapf
9901070 Paspalum L.
100   P. dilatatum Poir.
550   P. scrobiculatum L.
9901100 Urochloa Beauv.
400   U. mosambicensis (Hack.) Dandy
9901150 Oplismenus Beauv.
200   O. hirtellus (L.) Beauv.
9901160 Panicum L.
800   P. coloratum L. var. coloratum
1200   P. dregeanum Nees
2800   P. maximum Jacq.
3100   P. natalense Hochst.
9901280 Setaria Beauv.
1050   S. incrassata (Hochst.) Hack.
1200   S. lindenbergiana (Nees)
        Stapf
1500   S. nigrirostis (Nees) Dur. &
        Schinz
1800   S. pallide-fusca (Schumach.)
        Stapf & C.E. Hubb.
2450   S. saggittifolia (A. Rich.) Walp.
2500   S. sphacelata (Schumach.)
        Moss var. sphacelata
2590   S. sphacelata (Schumach.) Moss
        var. torta (Stapf) Clayton

3200   S. verticillata (L.) Beauv.
9901330 Tricholaena Schrad. ex
        Schult.
300   T. monachne (Trin.) Stapf &
        C.E. Hubb.
9901340 Melinis Beauv.
250   M. nerviglume (Franch.) Zizka
275   M. repens (Willd.) Zizka subsp.
        repens
9901380 Anthephora Schreb.
300   A. pubescens Nees
9901400 Cenchrus L.
300   C. ciliaris L.
9901730 Arundinella Raddi
100   A. nepalensis Trin.
9901740 Tristachya Nees
100   T. biseriata Stapf
450   T. leucothrix Nees
600   T. rehmannii Hack.
9901751 Loudetia Steud.
600   L. simplex (Nees) C.E. Hubb.
9902140 Phragmites Adanson.
100   P. australis (Cav.) Steud.
9902600 Stipagrostis Nees
3200   S. uniplumis (Licht.) De Winter
        var. uniplumis
9902620 Aristida L.
50   A. adscensionis L.
200   A. aequiglumis Hack.
500   A. canescens Henr. subsp.
        canescens
800   A. congesta Roem. & Schult.
        subsp. barbicollis (Trin. &
        Rupr.) De Winter
850   A. congesta Roem. & Schult.
        subsp. congesta
1200   A. diffusa Trin. subsp. burkei
        (Stapf) Melderis
2000   A. junciformis Trin. & Rupr.
        subsp. junciformis
2100   A. meridionalis Henr.
2700   A. rhiniochloa Hochst.
2900   A. scabrivalvis Hack. subsp.
        scabrivalvis
3300   A. stipitata Hack. subsp.
        graciliflora (Pilg.) Meld.
3550   A. stipitata Hack. subsp.
        stipitata
3700   A. transvaalensis Henr.
9902740 Tragus Haller
100   T. berteronianus Schult.
9902800 Perotis Aiton
200   P. patens Gand.
9902830 Sporobolus R. Br.
200   S. africanus (Poir.) Robyns &
        Tournay
1400   S. fimbriatus (Trin.) Nees
1700   S. ioclados (Trin.) Nees
2300   S. nitens Stent
2400   S. panicoides A. Rich.
2700   S. pyramidalis Beauv.
9902860 Eragrostis Wolf
100   E. acraea De Winter
600   E. aspera (Jacq.) Nees
1500   E. capensis (Thunb.) Trin.
1700   E. chloromelas Steud.
2300   E. curvula (Schrad.) Nees
3200   E. gummiflua Nees
3550   E. inamoena K.Schum.
4000   E. lappula Nees

4300	E. lehmanniana Nees var. lehmanniana
5000	E. nindensis Fical. & Hiern
5300	E. pallens Hack.
5800	E. plana Nees
6700	E. racemosa (Thunb.) Steud.
6900	E. rigidior Pilg.
8500	E. trichophora Coss. & Dur.
8900	E. viscosa (Retz.) Trin.
9902940	Microchloa R. Br.
100	M. caffra Nees
9902960	Cynodon Rich.
300	C. dactylon (L.) Pers.
9902980	Harpochloa Kunth
100	H. falx (L. f.) Kuntze
9903010	Chloris Swartz
200	C. gayana Kunth
350	C. pycnothrix Trin.
600	C. virgata Swartz
9903020	Eustachys Desv.
200	E. paspaloides (Vahl) Lanza & Mattei
9903310	Eleusine Gaertn.
300	E. indica (L.) Gaertn. subsp. indica
9903320	Dactyloctenium
100	D. aegyptim (L.) Willd.
9903340	Pogonarthria Stapf
300	P. squarrosa (Roem. & Schutl.) Pilg.
9903442	Bewsia Goossens
100	B. biflora (Hack.) Goossens
9903500	Triraphis R. Br.
100	T. andropogonoides (Steud.) Phill.
9903530	Trichoneura Anderss.
200	T. grandiglumis (Nees) Ekman var. grandiglumis
9903570	Enneapogon Beauv.
100	E. cenchroides (Roem. & Schult.) C.E. Hubb.
300	E. pretoriensis Stent
500	E. scoparius Stapf
9903610	Schmidtia Steud.
200	S. pappophoroides Steud.

CYPERACEAE

0454000	Ascolepis Nees ex Steud.
100	A. capensis (Kunth) Ridley
0459000	Cyperus L.
100	C. albostriatus Schrad.
300	C. amabilis Vahl
1200	C. denudatus L. f.
1900	C. esculentus L.
3400	C. leptocladus Kunth
3900	C. margaritaceus Vahl var. margaritaceus
4700	C. obtusiflorus Vahl var. flavissimus (Schrad.) Boeck.
4700	C. obtusiflorus Vahl. var. obtusiflorus
6400	C. rupestris Kunth var. rupestris
6500	C. schlechteri C.B. Clarke
7000	C. sphaerospermus Schrad.
8200	C. thorncroftii McClean
0459010	Pycreus Beauv.
700	P. flavescens (L.) Rchb.

1700	P. pelophilus (Ridl.) C.B. Clarke
0459030	Mariscus Gaertn.
500	M. congestus (Vahl) C.B. Cl.
1900	M. macer Kunth
2600	M. rehmannianus C.B. Cl.
0462000	Kyllinga Rottb.
200	K. alba Nees
0465000	Ficinia Schrad.
5300	Ficinia stolonifera Boeck.
0468000	Scirpus L.
1500	Scirpus ficinioides Kunth
0476000	Fuirena Rottb.
1100	F. pubescens (Poir.) Kunth
0471000	Fimbristylis Vahl
600	F. ferruginea L. (Vahl)
0471010	Bulbostylis Kunth
400	B. burchellii (Fical. & Hiern.) C.B. Cl.
0512000	Coleochloa Gilly
300	C. setifera (Ridley) Gilly
0525000	Carex L.
2000	C. spicato-paniculata C.B. Cl.

ARACEAE

0764000	Stylochiton Lepr.
100	S. natalense Schott

XYRIDACEAE

0826000	Xyris L.
300	X. congensis Büttner
400	X. gerrardii N.E. Br.
0828000	Eriocaulon L.
100	E. abyssinicum Hochst.
660	E. maculatum Schinz.

COMMELINACEAE

0896000	Commelina L.
100	C. africana L. var. africana
170	C africana L. var. lancispatha C.B. Cl.
300	C. benghalensis L.
700	C. erecta L.
1140	C. livingstonii C.B. Cl.
0904000	Cyanotis D. Don
200	C. lanata Benth.
300	C. lapidosa E. Phillips
500	C. speciosa (L. f.) Hassk.

COLCHICACEAE

0963000	Gloriosa L.
100	G. superba L.
0964000	Littonia Hook.
100	L. modesta Hook.
200	L. rigidifolia Bredell
0969000	Androcymbium Willd.
1700	A. longipes Baker

ASPHODELACEAE (PART A)

0985000	Bulbine Willd.
100	B. abyssinica A. Rich.
550	B. capitata V. Poelln.
1000	B. favosa (Thunb.) Schult. & Schult. f.
0985010	Trachyandra Kunth
3800	T. laxa (N.E. Br.) Oberm. var. rigida (Suess.) Roessler
4800	T. saltii (Bak.) Oberm. var. saltii

0989000	Anthericum L.
300	A. angulicaule Bak.
0990000	Chlorophytum Ker-Gawl
200	C. bowkeri Bak.

HYACINTHACEAE (PART A)

1011000	Bowiea Harv. ex Hook. f.
100	B. volubilis Harv. ex Hook. f.

ERIOSPERMACEAE

1012000	Eriospermum Jacq. ex Willd.
100	E. abyssinicum Bak.
2100	E. cooperi Bak.
5200	E. porphyrium Arch.

ASPHODELACEAE (PART B)

1024000	Kniphofia Moench
1000	K. coralligemma E.A. Bruce
1400	K. ensifolia Bak. subsp. ensifolia
1026000	Aloe L.
800	A. arborescens Mill.
2700	A. chabaudii Schonl.
4600	A. dolomitica Groenew.
5200	A. excelsa Berger
9700	A. marlothii Berger var. marlothii
12500	A. pretoriensis Pole Evans
13500	A. sessiliflora Pole Evans
15600	A. transvaalensis Kuntze

ALLIACEAE

1046000	Agapanthus L'Herit
100	A. africanus (L.) Hoffmg.
700	A. coddii Leight.

HYACINTHACEAE (PART B)

1079000	Albuca L.
2900	A. glauca Bak.
5200	A. setosa Jacq.
1080000	Urginea Steinh.
3100	U. sanguinea Schinz
1084000	Dipcadi Medik.
500	D. glaucum (Ker-Gawl.) Bak.
1086000	Scilla L.
300	S. nervosa (Burch.) Jessop
1088000	Eucomis L'Herit.
300	E. autumnalis (Mill.) Chitt. subsp. clavata (Bak.) Reyneke
1089000	Ornithogalum L.
3200	O. juncifolium Jacq.
6300	O. seineri (Engl. & Krause). Oberm.
6940	O. tenuifolium F. Delaroche subsp. tenuifolium
1090000	Drimiopsis Lindl.
200	D. burkei Bak.
1090010	Ledebouria Roth.
300	L. cooperi (Hook. f.) Jessop
500	L. graminifolia (Baker) Jessop
1100	L. ovalifolia (Bak.) Jessop

DRACAENACEAE

1110000	Sansevieria Thunb.
200	S. hyacinthoides (L.) Druce
300	S. pearsonii N.E. Br.

ASPARAGACEAE
1113010 Asparagus Oberm.
        A. angusticladus (Jessop)
        J.-P. Lebrun & Stork
        A. asparagoides (L.) Druce
3100   A. krebsianus (Kunth) Oberm.
        A. racemosus Willd.
5900   A. setaceus (Kunth) Oberm.
6300   A. suaveolens (Burch.) Oberm.
        A. virgatus (Bak.) Oberm.

AMARYLLIDACEAE
1167000 Haemanthus L.
1800   H. humilis Jacq. subsp. humilis
1167010 Scadoxus Raf.
400   S. puniceus (L.) Friis & Nordal
1168000 Boophane Herb.
100   B. disticha (L. f.) Herb.
1177000 Brunsvigia Heist.
1100   B. natalensis Bak.
1400   B. radulosa Herb.
1189000 Crinum L.
400   C. buphanoides Welw. ex Bak.
1190000 Ammocharis Herb.
100   A. coranica (Ker-Gawl.) Herb.
1191000 Cyrtanthus L. f.
4400   C. stenanthus Baker var.
        major R.A. Dyer
1202000 Pancratium L.
100   P. tenuifolium Hochst. ex A.
        Rich.

HYPOXIDACEAE
1230000 Hypoxis L.
200   H. angustifolia Lam. var.
        angustifolia
1500   H. filiformis Bak.
1800   H. galpinii Bak.
2200   H. iridifolia Bak.
4200   H. rigidula Bak. var. rigidula

TECOPHILAEACEAE
1231000 Walleria Kirk
200   W. nutans Kirk

VELLOZIACEAE
1247010 Xerophyta Juss.
400   X. retinervis Bak.
800   X. viscosa Bak.

IRIDACEAE
1265000 Moraea Mill.
7455   M. thomsonii Bak.
1295000 Aristea Ait.
4200   A. woodii N.E. Br.
1299000 Schizostylis Backh. & Harv.
100   S. coccinea Backh. & Harv.
1301000 Hesperantha Ker-Gawl.
550   H. bulbifera Baker
600   H. candida Baker
1303000 Dierama K. Koch.
1500   D. medium N.E. Br.
1306000 Tritonia Ker-Gawl.
2100   T. nelsonii Bak.
1306010 Crocosmia Planch.
100   C. aurea (Pappe ex Hook.)
        Planch. var. aurea
1310000 Babiana Ker-Gawl.
2400   B. hypogea Burch. var.
        hypogea

1311000 Gladiolus L.
1100   G. atropurpureus Bak.
3300   G. crassifolius Bak.
3550   G. dalenii Van Geel
4000   G. ecklonii Lehm. subsp.
        ecklonii
4300   G. elliotii Bak.
9600   G. permeabilis D. Delaroche
        subsp. edulis (Burch. ex Ker
        Gawl.) Oberm.
10200   G. pretoriensis Kuntze
11700   G. sericeovillosus Hook. f.
        subsp. calvatus (Baker)
        Goldblatt
14100   G. woodii Bak.
1314000 Lapeirousia Pourret
2950   L. sandersonii Bak.
1316010 Anomatheca Ker-Gawl.
200   A. grandiflora Bak.

ORCHIDACEAE
1407000 Stenoglottis Lindl.
100   S. fimbriata Lindl.
1408000 Holothrix L.C. Rich. ex Hook.
1600   H. orthoceras (Harv.) Reichb. f.
1422000 Habenaria Willd.
1250   H. falciformis (Burch. ex
        Lindl.) H. Bol. var. caffra
        (Schltr.) J.C. Manning
1430000 Satyrium Swartz
1300   S. cristatum Sond. var.
        cristatum
3900   S. parviflorum Sw.
5050   S. trinerve Lindl.
1434000 Disa Berg.
3600   D. nervosa Lindl.
        Lower Risk LR-lc
4300   D. patula Sond. var.
        transvaalensis Summerh.
4500   D. polygonoides Lindl.
5400   D. saxicola Schltr.
7200   D. woodii Schltr.
        Lower Risk LR-lc
1435010 Herschelianthe Rauschert
300   H. baurii (H. Bol.) Rauschert
1437000 Disperis Swartz
2300   D. micrantha Lindl.
1568000 Ansellia Lindl.
20   A. africana Lindl.
        Lower Risk LR-nt
1648000 Eulophia R. Br. ex Lindl.
300   E. angolensis (Reichb. f.)
        Summerh.
1000   E. coddii A.V. Hall
2700   E. ovalis Lindl. subsp. bainesii
        (Rolfe) A.V. Hall
2800   E. ovalis Lindl. subsp. ovalis
3100   E. petersii (Rchb. f.) Rchb. f.
3500   E. streptopetala Lindl.
3900   E. welwitchii (Reichb. f.) Rolfe

DICOTYLEDONAE

ULMACEAE
1898000 Celtis L.
100   C. africana Burm. f.
1902000 Trema Lour.
100   T. orientalis (L.) Blume
1906000 Chaetacme Planch.
100   C. aristata Planch.

MORACEAE
1961000 Ficus L.
1000   F. glumosa (Miq.) Del.
1200   F. ingens (Miq.) Miq. var.
        ingens
2250   F. sur Forssk.
2450   F. thonningii Blume

URTICACEAE
1979000 Obetia Gaudich.
200   O. tenax (N.E. Br.) Friis
1992000 Pouzolzia Gaudich.
100   P. mixta Solms

PROTEACEAE
2034000 Faurea Harv.
300   F. saligna Harv.
2035000 Protea L.
1200   P. caffra Meisn. subsp.
        caffra
3000   P. gaguedi Gmel.
7300   P. roupelliae Meisn. subsp.
        roupelliae
9150   P. welwitschii Engl.

LORANTHACEAE
2074010 Tapinanthus Reichb.
1100   T. leendertziae (Sprague)
        Wiens
1500   T. natalitius (Meisn.) Danser
        subsp. zeyheri (Harv.) Wiens
1600   T. oleifolius (Wendl.) Danser
1800   T. rubromarginatus (Engl.)
        Danser

VISCACEAE
2093000 Viscum L.
300   V. combreticola Engl.
1700   V. rotundifolium L. f.
1870   V. spragueanum Burtt Davy
2200   V. verrucosum Harv.

SANTALACEAE
2108000 Osyris L.
100   O. lanceolata Hochst. &
        Steud.
2118000 Thesium L.
3400   T. cytisoides A.W. Hill
6500   T. goetzeanum Engl.
9800   T. magalismontanum Sond.
13500   T. racemosum Bernh.
16700   T. utile A.W. Hill

OLACACEAE
2131000 Olax L.
100   O. dissitiflora Oliv.
2136000 Ximenia L.
150   X. americana L. var.
        americana
300   X. caffra Sond. var. caffra

POLYGONACEAE
2201030 Persicaria Mill.
200   P. attenuata (R. Br.) Sojak
        subsp. africana K.L. Wilson
1200   P. serulata (Lag.) Webb. &
        Moq.

CHENOPODIACEAE
2269000 Salsola L.
800 S. aphylla L. f.
5600 S. rabieana I. Verd.

AMARANTHACEAE
2293000 Hermbstaedtia Reichb.
400 H. odorata (Burch.) T. Cooke
var. odorata
370 H. odorata (Burch.) T. Cooke
var. aurantiaca (Suess.) C.C.
Towns.
2309000 Kyphocarpa (Fenzl) Lopr.
100 K. angustifolia (Moq.) Lopr.
2312000 Cyathula Blume
300 C. cylindrica Moq. var.
cylindrica
2328000 Achyranthes L.
100 A. aspera L. var. aspera
175 A. aspera L. var. sicula L.
2328020 Achyropsis (Moq.) Hook. f.
200 A. leptostachya (E. Mey. Ex
Meisn.) Baker & C.B. Clarke
2330010 Guilleminea Kunth.
100 G. densa (Willd. ex Roem. &
Schult.) Moq.
2335000 Alternanthera Forssk.
400 A. sessilis (L.) DC.

AIZOACEAE (PART A)
2376000 Limeum L.
1400 L. fenestratum (Fenzl)
Heimerl var. fenestratum
2900 L. viscosum (J. Gay) Fenzl
subsp. viscosum var. dubium
Friedr.
3000 L. viscosum (J. Gay) Fenzl
subsp. viscosum var.
glomeratum (Eckl. & Zeyh.)
Friedrich
2379000 Psammotropha Eckl. & Zeyh.
600 P. mucronata (Thunb.) Fenzl
var. foliosa Adamson
800 P. mucronata (Thunb.) Fenzl
var. mucronata
900 P. myriantha Sond.

PHYTOLACCACEAE (PART B)
2380000 Phytolacca L.
500 P. octandra L.

GISEKIACEAE
2382000 Gisekia L.
300 G. pharnacioides L. var.
pharnacioides

PORTULACACEAE
2406000 Talinum Adans.
200 T. caffrum (Thunb.) Eckl. &
Zeyh.
2412000 Anacampseros L.
2400 A. subnuda V. Poelln.
2421000 Portulaca L.
600 P. kermesina N.E. Br.

CARYOPHYLLACEAE (PART A)
2455000 Polycarpaea Lam.
100 P. corymbosa (L.) Lam.

ILLECEBRACEAE
2467000 Pollichia Ait.
100 P. campestris Ait.

CARYOPHYLLACEAE (PART B)
2502000 Dianthus L.
1600 D. mooiensis F.N. Williams
subsp. mooiensis var.
mooiensis
1400 D. mooiensis F.N. Williams
subsp. Kirkii (Burtt Davy)
Hooper

NYMPHAEACEAE
2513000 Nymphaea L.
530 N. nouchali Burm. f. var.
carulea (Sav.) Verdc.

RANUNCULACEAE
2542000 Clematis L.
100 C. brachiata Thunb.
200 C. oweniae Harv.
2542010 Clematopsis Boj. ex Hutch.
100 C. scabiosifolia (D.C.) Hutch.
subsp. stanleyi
(Hook.) Brummitt

ANNONACEAE
2716000 Hexalobus A. DC.
100 H. monopetalus (A. Rich.)
Engl. & Diels var. monopetalus

CAPPARACEAE
3082000 Cleome L.
900 C. gynandra L.
1000 C. hirta (Klotzsch) Oliv.
1500 C. maculata (Sond.) Szyszyl.
2000 C. rubella Burch.
3106000 Boscia Lam.
100 B. albitrunca Gilg. & Ben. var.
albitrunca
300 B. foetida Schinz. subsp.
foetida
3109000 Cadaba Forssk.
100 C. aphylla (Thunb.) Wild
400 C. termitaria N.E. Br.
3112000 Maerua Forssk.
100 M. angolensis DC.

DROSERACEAE
3136000 Drosera L.
1300 D. madagascariensis DC.

CRASSULACEAE
3164000 Cotyledon L.
3230 C. orbiculata L. var. oblonga
(Haw.) DC.
3165000 Bryophylum Salisb.
100 B. delagoense (Eckl. & Zeyh.)
Schinz.
3166000 Kalanchoe Adans.
1400 K. lanceolata (Forssk.) Pers.
2100 K. paniculata Harv.
2700 K. rotundifolia (Haw.) Haw.
3450 K. sexangularis N.E. Br.
3168000 Crassula L.
300 C. alba Forssk. var. alba
5100 C. capitata Thunb. subsp.
nodulosa (Schonl.) Tölken
8070 C. cymbiformis Toelken

11800 C. expansa Dryand. subsp.
fragilis (Bak.) Tölken
16000 C. lanceolata (Eckl. & Zeyh.)
Endl. ex Walp. subsp.
lanceolata
23400 C. perfoliata L. var.
heterotricha (Schinz) Tölken
26900 C. sarcocaulis Eckl. & Zeyh.
subsp. sarcocaulis
30955 C. swaziensis Schonl.

VAHLIACEAE
3201000 Vahlia Thunb.
100 V. capensis (L. f.) Thunb.
subsp. capensis

PITTOSPORACEAE
3252000 Pittosporum Banks ex
Gaertn.
300 P. viridiflorum Sims

MYROTHAMNACEAE
3282000 Myrothamnus Welw.
100 M. flabellifolius Welw.

ROSACEAE (PART A)
3353000 Rubus L.
1300 R. rigidus Sm.
3388000 Cliffortia L.
5800 C. linearifolia Eckl. & Zeyh.

CHRYSOBALANACEAE
3405000 Parinari Aubl.
100 P. capensis Harv. subsp.
capensis

FABACEAE
3443000 Albizia Durazz.
500 A. brevifolia Schinz
1000 A. tanganyicensis Bak. f.
subsp. tanganyicensis
3446000 Acacia Mill.
90300 A. ataxacantha DC.
90600 A. burkei Benth.
90700 A. caffra (Thunb.) Willd.
91100 A. erubescens Welw. ex Oliv.
91500 A. gerrardii Benth. var.
gerrardii
92300 A. karroo Hayne
93400 A. nilotica (L.) Willd. ex Del.
subsp. kraussiana (Benth.)
Brenan
93500 A. permixta Burtt Davy
94100 A. robusta Burch. subsp.
robusta
95000 A. tortilis (Forssk.) Hayne
subsp. heteracantha (Burch.)
Brenan
3452000 Dichrostachys (A. DC.) Wight
& Arn.
100 D. cinerea (L.) Wight & Arn.
subsp. africana Brenan &
Brumm. var. africana
3467000 Elephantorrhiza Benth.
100 E. burkei Benth.
200 E. elephantina (Burch.) Skeels
600 E. obliqua Burtt Davy var.
glabra E. Phillips
3474000 Burkea Benth.

100	B. africana Hook.
3506000	Schotia Jacq.
300	S. brachypetala Sond.
3536010	Chamaecrista Moench
100	C. absus (L.) Irwin & Barneby
200	C. biensis (Steyaert) Lock
500	C. comosa E. Mey. var. capricornia (Steyaert) Lock
600	C. comosa E. Mey. var. comosa
800	C. mimosoides (L.) Greene
3536020	Senna Mill.
900	S. occidentalis (L.) Link
3561000	Peltophorum (Vogel) Benth.
100	P. africanum Sond.
3607000	Calpurnia E. Mey.
100	C. aurea (Ait.) Benth. subsp. aurea
3657000	Lotononis DC.
1800	L. calycina (E. Mey.) Benth.
3400	L. eriantha Benth.
4900	L. laxa Eckl. & Zeyh.
5150	L. listii Polhill
3657010	Pearsonia Dümmer
400	P. cajanifolia (Harv.) Polhill subsp. cryptantha (Bak.) Polhill
1000	P. sessilifolia (Harv.) Dümmer subsp. sessilifolia
3669000	Crotalaria L.
4700	C. orientalis Burtt Davy ex Verdoorn subsp. orientalis
5300	C. pisicarpa Welw. ex Baker
5500	C. podocarpa DC.
6800	C. sphaerocarpa Perr. ex DC. subsp. sphaerocarpa
3673000	Argyrolobium Eckl. & Zeyh.
2400	A. pauciflorum Eckl. & Zeyh. var. pauciflorum
3800	A. transvaalense Schinz
3702000	Indigofera L.
300	I. adenoides Bak. f.
3800	I. comosa N.E. Br.
5200	I. daleoides Benth. ex Harv. var. daleoides
7100	I. egens N.E. Br.
8300	I. filipes Benth. ex Harv.
8500	I. flavicans Baker
10500	I. hedyantha Eckl. & Zeyh.
10800	I. hilaris Eckl. & Zeyh.
13900	I. melanadenia Benth. ex Harv.
14400	I. mollicoma N.E. Br.
15900	I. oxalidea Welw. ex Bak.
22500	I. vicioides Jaub. & Spach var. vicioides
3703040	Otholobium C.H. Stirton
2400	O. polystictum (Benth. ex Harv.) C.H. Stirt.
3717010	Ptycholobium Harms.
400	P. plicatum (Oliv.) Harms subsp. plicatum
3718000	Tephrosia Pers.
1200	T. capensis (Jacq.) Pers. var. capensis
2200	T. elongata E. Mey. var. elongata
4400	T. longipes Meisn. subsp. longipes
6700	T. purpurea (L.) Pers. subsp.

	leptostachya (DC.) Brummitt var. leptostachya
6750	T. purpurea (L.) Pers. subsp. leptostachya (DC.) Brummitt var. pubescens Baker
7200	T. rhodesica Bak. f. var. rhodesica
3719000	Mundulea (DC.) Benth.
100	M. sericea (Willd.) A. Chev.
3793000	Aeschynomene L.
900	A. rehmannii Shinz var. leptobotrya (Harms ex Bak. f.) J.B. Gillet
3802000	Stylosanthes Swartz
100	S. fruticosa (Retz.) Alston
3804000	Zornia J.F. Gmel.
300	Z. linearis E. Mey.
400	Z. milneana Mohlenbr.
3828000	Pterocarpus Jacq.
400	P. rotundifolius (Sond.) Druce subsp. rotundifolius
3864010	Neonotonia Lackey
100	N. wightii (Arn.) J.A. Lackey
3856000	Abrus Adans.
100	A. laevigatus E. Mey.
200	A. precatorius L. subsp. africanus Verdc.
3870000	Erythrina L.
900	E. lysistemon Hutch.
3808000	Pseudarthria Wight & Arn.
100	P. hookeri Wight & Arn. var. hookeri
3891000	Canavalia D.C.
600	C. virosa (Roxb.) Wight & Arn.
3897000	Rhynchosia Lour.
100	R. adenodes Eckl. & Zeyh.
2100	R. densiflora (Roth) DC. subsp. chrysadenia (Taub.) Verdc.
4400	R. monophylla Schltr.
4700	R. nitens Benth.
5750	R. resinosa (A. Rich.) Baker
6500	R. spectabilis Schinz
7000	R. totta (Thunb.) DC. var. totta
3898000	Eriosema (DC.) G. Don
300	E. burkei Benth.
400	E. cordatum E. Mey.
700	E. ellipticifolium Schinz
1410	E. psoraleoides (Lam.) G. Don
1600	E. salignum E. Mey.
3905000	Vigna Savi
2000	V. unguiculata (L.) Walp. subsp. unguiculata
3906000	Otoptera DC.
100	O. burchellii DC.
3907000	Sphenostylis E. Mey.
100	S. angustifolia Sond.
3909000	Lablab Adans.
200	L. purpureus (L.) Sweet subsp. uncinatus Verdc.
3910000	Dolichos L.
1200	D. pratensis (E. Mey.) Taub.

GERANIACEAE

3925000	Monsonia L.
200	M. angustifolia E. Mey. ex A. Rich.
3928000	Pelargonium L'Hèrit.
7200	P. graveolens L'Hér.

9700	P. luridum (Andr.) Sweet

OXALIDACEAE

3936000	Oxalis L.
5300	O. depressa Eckl. & Zeyh.
14800	O. obliquifolia Steud. ex Rich.
19500	O. semiloba Sond. subsp. semiloba

ZYGOPHYLLACEAE

3956000	Erythroxylum P. Br
200	E. emarginatum Thonn.
3978000	Tribulus L.
400	T. terrestris L.

RUTACEAE

3991000	Zanthoxylum L.
100	Z. capense (Thunb.) Harv.
4035000	Calodendrum Thunb.
100	C. capense (L. f.) Thunb.
4076000	Vepris Comm. ex A. Juss.
150	V. lanceolata (Lam.) G. Don

SIMAROUBACEAE

4128000	Kirkia Oliv.
300	K. wilmsii Engl.

BURSERACEAE

4151000	Commiphora Jacq.
100	C. africana (A. Rich.) Engl.
1100	C. glandulosa Schinz
1800	C. mollis (Oliv.) Engl.

MELIACEAE (PART B)

4171000	Turraea L.
200	T. obtusifolia Hochst.
4175000	Melia L.
100	M. azedarach L.

MALPIGHIACEAE

4206000	Triaspis Burch.
100	T. glaucophylla Engl.
250	T. hypericoides (DC.) Burch. subsp. nelsonii (Oliv.) Immelman
4219000	Sphedamnocarpus Planch. ex Benth. & Hook. f.
500	S. pruriens (Juss.) Szyszyl. subsp. pruriens

POLYGALACEAE

4273000	Polygala L.
200	P. africana Chodat
400	P. amatymbica Eckl. & Zeyh.
2450	P. gracilenta Burtt Davy
2900	P. hottentotta Presl
6900	P. sphenoptera Fresen. var. sphenoptera
7300	P. uncinata E. Mey. ex Meisn.
7400	P. virgata Thunb. var. decora (Sond.) Harv.
4275000	Securidaca L.
100	S. longepedunculata Fresen.

EUPHORBIACEAE

4295000	Pseudolachnostylis Pax
150	P. maprouneifolia Pax var. dekindtii (Pax) Radcliffe-Sm.
4297000	Flueggea Comm. ex Juss.
100	F. virosa (Roxb. ex Willd.) Pax & K. Hoffm.

4299000	Phyllanthus L.	7480	R. tumulicola S. Moore var. tumulicola	700	G. flavescens Juss. var. flavescens
1500	P. maderaspatensis L.	7500	R. undulata Jacq.	800	G. flavescens Juss. var. olukondae (Schinz) Wild
2100	P. parvulus Sond.				
2200	P. pentandrus Schumach. & Thonn.	**AQUIFOLIACEAE**		1600	G. monticola Sond.
4345000	Bridelia Willd.	4614000	Ilex L.	1700	G. occidentalis L.
500	B. mollis Hutch.	100	I. mitis (L.) Radlk. var. mitis	2000	G. rogersii Burtt Davy & Greenway
4348000	Croton L.				
200	C. gratissimus Burch. var. grattisimus	**CELASTRACEAE**		2200	G. subspathulata N.E. Br.
		4626000	Maytenus Molina	4975000	Triumfetta L.
300	C. gratissimus Burch. var. subgratissimus (Prain) Burtt Davy	400	M. heterophylla (Eckl. & Zeyh.) N.K.B. Robson	600	T. pentandra A. Rich. var. pentandra
		1300	M. polyacantha (Sond.) Marais	1100	T. sonderi Ficalho & Hiern.
800	C. pseudopulchellus Pax	1600	M. senegalensis (Lam.) Exell		
4407000	Acalypha L.	1700	M. tenuispina (Sond.) Marais	**MALVACEAE**	
200	A. angustata Sond. var. glabra Sond.	1800	M. undata (Tunb.) Blakelock	4983000	Abutilon Mill.
		4630000	Pterocelastrus Meisn.	300	A. austro-africanum Hochr.
500	A. ciliata Forssk.	100	P. echinatus N.E. Br.	4998000	Sida L.
1600	A. peduncularis E. Mey. ex Meisn.	200	P. rostratus (Thunb.) Walp.	250	S. alba L.
		4641000	Cassine L.	400	S. cordifolia L.
4416000	Tragia L.	1200	C. transvaalensis (Burtt Davy) Codd	500	S. dregei Burtt Davy
1200	T. rupestris Sond.			700	S. ovata Forssk.
4422000	Dalechampia L.	4662000	Salacia L.	900	S. rhombifolia L.
100	D. capensis A. Spreng.	500	S. rehmannii Schinz	5007000	Pavonia Cav.
4433000	Jatropha L.			100	P. burchellii (DC.) R.A. Dyer
1800	J. zeyheri Sond. var. subsimplex Prain	**ICACINACEAE**		300	P. columella Cav.
		4671000	Cassinopsis Sond.	1200	P. transvaalensis (Ulbr.) A. Meeuse
4448000	Clutia L.	100	C. ilicifolia (Hochst.) Kuntze		
3200	C. pulchella L. var. pulchella	4686000	Apodytes E. Mey. ex Arn.	5013000	Hibiscus L.
4478000	Spirostachys Sond.	100	A. dimidiata E. Mey. ex Arn. subsp. dimidiata	1200	H. calyphyllus Cav.
100	S. africana Sond.			2200	H. engleri K. Schum.
4498000	Euphorbia L.			2800	H. lunarifolius Willd.
4400	E. clavarioides Boiss var. truncata (N.E. Br.) White, Dyer & Sloane	**SAPINDACEAE**		3500	H. micranthus L. f. var. micranthus
		4726000	Cardiospermum L.		
		100	C. corindum L.	4700	H. schinzii Gürke
5300	E. cooperi N.E. Br. ex Berger var. cooperi	4784000	Pappea Eckl. & Zeyh.	4300	H. pusillus Thunb.
		100	P. capensis Eckl. & Zeyh.	5300	H. trionum L.
5700	E. crotonoides Boiss. subsp. crotonoides				
		RHAMNACEAE		**STERCULIACEAE**	
13900	E. ingens E. Mey. ex Boiss.	4861000	Ziziphus Mill.	5053000	Dombeya Cav.
23200	E. schinzii Pax	100	Z. mucronata Willd. subsp. mucronata	600	D. rotundifolia (Hochst.) Planch. var. rotundifolia
26400	E. tricadenia Pax				
4498010	Chamaesyce S.F. Gray	4868000	Berchemia Neck. ex DC.	5056000	Hermannia L.
600	C. inaequilatera (Sond.) Soják	200	B. zeyheri (Sond.) Grubov	3100	H. boraginiflora Hook.
1000	C. neopolynemoides Pax & K. Hoffm.	4886000	Phylica L.	7100	H. depressa N.E. Br.
		11800	P. paniculata Willd.	12300	H. grisea Schinz
				28500	H. tomentosa (Turcz.) Schinz ex Engl.
BUXACEAE		**VITACEAE**			
4533000	Buxus L.	4917000	Rhoicissus Planch.	23200	H. quartiniana A. Rich. subsp. stellulata (K. Schum) De Winter
100	B. macowanii Oliv.	100	R. digitata (L. f.) Gilg & M. Brandt		
				5059000	Waltheria L.
ANACARDIACEAE		300	R. revoilii Planch.	100	W. indica L.
4558000	Sclerocarya Hochst.	550	R. tridentata (L. f.) Wild & Drum. subsp. cuneifolia (Eckl. & Zeyh.) N.R. Urton	5047000	Melhania Forssk.
100	S. birrea (A. Rich.) Hochst. subsp. caffra (Sond.) Kokwaro			100	M. acuminata Mast. var. acuminata
		4918000	Cissus L.		
4563000	Lannea A. Rich.	700	C. quadrangularis L.	700	M. forbesii Planch. ex Mast.
100	L. discolor (Sond.) Engl.	4918010	Cyphostemma (Planch.) Alston	1100	M. prostrata DC.
200	L. edulis (Sond.) Engl. var. edulis	1150	C. hardyi Retief		
		1800	C. lanigerum (Harv.) Descoings ex Wild & Drum.	**OCHNACEAE**	
4589010	Ozoroa Del.			5112000	Ochna L.
1100	O. paniculosa (Sond.) R. & A. Fernandes var. paniculosa			100	O. arborea Burch. ex DC. var. arborea
		TILIACEAE			
4594000	Rhus L.	4953000	Corchorus L.	600	O. holstii Engl.
1500	R. dentata Thunb.	200	C. asplenifolius Burch.	1100	O. pretoriensis Phill.
3000	R. gracillima Engl.	600	C. kirkii N.E. Br.	1200	O. pulchra Hook.
3900	R. lancea L. f.	4966000	Grewia L.		
4000	R. leptodictya Diels	100	G. avellana Hiern.		
4400	R. magalismontana Sond.	200	G. bicolor Juss.		
5600	R. pyroides Burch. var. pyroides	600	G. flava DC.		

CLUSIACEAE
5168000 Hypericum L.
100 H. aethiopicum Thunb. subsp. aethiopicum
200 H. aethiopicum Thunb. subsp. sonderi (Bredell) N. Robson
400 H. lalandii Choisy

FLACOURTIACEAE
5304000 Scolopia Schreb.
500 S. zeyheri (Nees) Harv.
5327000 Flacourtia Comm. ex L'Hérit.
100 F. indica (Burm. f.) Merr.
532800 Dovyalis E. Mey. ex Arn.
700 D. zeyheri (Sond.) Warb.

TURNERACEAE
5356000 Streptopetalum Hochst.
100 S. serratum Hochst.
5357000 Piriqueta Aubl.
100 P. capensis (Harv.) Urb.

PASSIFLORACEAE
5370000 Adenia Forssk.
500 A. glauca Schinz

CACTACEAE
5417000 Opuntia Mill.
400 O. ficus-indica (L.) Mill.

OLINIACEAE
5428000 Olinia Thunb.
300 O. rochetiana Juss.

THYMELAEACEAE
5435000 Gnidia L.
320 G. caffra (Meisn.) Gilg
500 G. capitata L. f.
2700 G. kraussiana Meisn. var. kraussiana
5461000 Passerina L.
810 P. montana Thoday

LYTHRACEAE
5473000 Rotala L.
R. sp.
5486000 Nesea Comm. Ex Juss.
300 N. cordata Hiern.

COMBRETACEAE
5538000 Combretum Loefl.
200 C. apiculatum Sond. subsp. apiculatum
1400 C. erythrophyllum (Burch.) Sond.
1500 C. hereroense Schinz
1700 C. imberbe Wawra
1800 C. kraussii Hochst.
2000 C. moggii Exell
2100 C. molle R. Br. ex G. Don
3200 C. zeyheri Sond.
5544000 Terminalia L.
100 T. brachystemma Welw. ex Hiern
500 T. sericea Burch. ex DC.

MYRTACEAE
5583000 Syzygium Gaertn.
100 S. cordatum Hochst.
400 S. guineense (Willd.) DC.

500 S. intermedium Engl. & Brehmer
5588010 Heteropyxis Harv.
100 H. natalensis Harv.

MELASTOMATACEAE
5651000 Antheromata Hook. f.
100 A. naudinii Hook. f.
5659000 Dissotis Benth.
300 D. debilis (Sond.) Triana var. debilis D. sp.

ARALIACEAE
5872000 Cussonia Thunb.
450 C. paniculata Eckl. & Zeyh. subsp. sinuata (Reyneke & Kok) De Winter
600 C. spicata Thunb.
750 C. transvaalensis Reyneke

APIACEAE
5992000 Heteromorpha Cham. & Schlectd.
600 H. trifoliata (Wendl.) Eckl. & Zeyh.

CORNACEAE
6156000 Curtisia Ait.
100 C. dentata (Burm. f.) C.A. Sm.

ERICACEAE
6237000 Erica L.
19800 E. drakensbergensis Guth. & Bol.

MYRSINACEAE
6313000 Myrsine L.
100 M. africana L.

PLUMBAGINACEAE
6343000 Plumbago L.
500 P. zeylanica L.

SAPOTACEAE
6377010 Englerophytum De Wild.
100 E. magalismontanum (Sond.) Heine & J.H. Hemsl.
6386000 Mimusops L.
300 M. zeyheri Sond.

EBENACEAE
6404000 Euclea Murray
400 E. crispa (Thunb.) Guerke subsp. crispa
800 E. linearis Zeyh. ex Hiern
1000 E. natalensis A. DC. subsp. natalensis
1075 E. polyandra (L. f.) E. Mey. ex Hiern
1700 E. undulata Thunb. var. undulata
6406000 Diospyros L.
1300 D. lycioides Desf. subsp. guerkei (Kuntze) De Winter
1400 D. lycioides Desf. subsp. lycioides
2900 D. whyteana (Hiern) F. White

OLEACEAE
6422000 Schrebera Roxb.
100 S. alata (Hochst.) Welw.
6434000 Olea L.
300 O. capensis L. subsp. enervis (Harv. ex C.H. Wr.) Verdoorn
450 O. europaea L. subsp. africana (Mill.) P.S. Green
6440000 Jasminum L.
600 J. multipartitum Hochst.

LOGANIACEAE
6460000 Strychnos L.
100 S. cocculoides Bak.
400 S. madagascariensis Poir.
700 S. pungens Soler.
900 S. usambarensis Gilg
6469000 Nuxia Comm. ex Lam.
100 N. congesta R. Br. ex Fresen.
200 N. floribunda Benth.

BUDDLEJACEAE
6473000 Buddleja
700 B. salviifolia (l.) Lam.

GENTIANACEAE
6481000 Sebaea Soland. ex R. Br.
1700 S. grandis (E. Mey.) Steud.
2000 S. junodii Schinz
2200 S. leiostyla Gilg
6503000 Chironia L.
1400 C. palustris Burch. subsp. transvaalensis (Gilg) Verdoorn
1700 C. purpurascens (E. Mey.) Benth. & Hook. f. subsp. humilis (Gilg) Verdoorn

APOCYNACEAE
6558000 Acokanthera G. Don
200 A. oppositifolia (Lam.) Codd
6559000 Carissa L.
200 C. bispinosa (L.) Desf. ex Brenan subsp. bispinosa
6562020 Ancylobotrys Pierre
100 A. capensis (Oliv.) Pichon
6589000 Diplorhynchus Welw. ex Fical. & Hiern
100 D. condylocarpon (MÜll. Arg.) Pichon

PERIPLOCACEAE
6740000 Cryptolepis R. Br.
200 C. oblongifolia (Meisn.) Schltr.
400 C. transvaalensis Schltr.
6747000 Raphionacme Harv.
100 R. burkei N.E. Br.
500 R. galpinii Schltr.

ASCLEPIADACEAE
6777000 Xysmalobium R. Br.
1500 X. undulatum (L.) Ait. f.
6787010 Pachycarpus E. Mey.
2700 P. schinzianus (Schltr.) N.E. Br.
6791000 Asclepias L.
400 A. aurea (Schltr.) Schltr.
3100 A. fruticosa L.
6810000 Pentarrhinum E. Mey.
300 P. insipidum E. Mey.

6849000 Sarcostemma R. Br.
100 S. viminale (L.) R. Br.
6860000 Secamone R. Br.
100 S. alpini Schult.
300 S. filiformis (L. f.) J.H. Ross
6860000 S. parvifolia (Oliv.) Bullock
6874000 Ceropegia L.
C. sp
6885000 Stapelia L.
4400 S. gigantea N.E. Br.
6885070 Orbeopsis Leach
700 O. lutea (N.E. Br.) Leach
subsp. lutea
6917000 Pergularia L.
100 P. daemia (Forssk.) Chiov. var.
daemia

CONVOLVULACEAE
6973000 Evolvulus L.
100 E. alsinoides (L.) L. var.
linifolius (L.) Bak.
6978000 Seddera Hocst.
100 S. capensis (E. Mey. ex
Choisy) Hallier f.
6993000 Convolvulus L.
1800 C. sagittatus Thunb. subsp.
sagittatus var. hirtellus
(Hallier f.) A. Meeuse
6997000 Merremia Dennst.
700 M. pinnata (Hochst. ex
Choisy) Hallier f.
900 M. tridentata (L.) Hallier f.
subsp. angustifolia (Jacq.)
Van Oostr. var. angustifolia
7003000 Ipomoea L.
300 I. albivenia (Lindl.) Sweet
800 I. bathycolpos Hallier f.
1100 I. bolusiana Schinz subsp.
bolusiana
1700 I. crassipes Hook.
2800 I. magnusiana Schinz var.
eenii (Rendle) A. Meeuse
3300 I. obscura (L.) Ker-Gawl. var.
obscura
3500 I. ommaneyi Rendle
5000 I. transvaalensis A. Meeuse
7008010 Turbina Rafin.
50 T. holubii (Bak.) A. Meeuse

BORAGINACEAE
7043000 Ehretia P.Br.
200 E. rigida (Thunb.) Druce
7052000 Heliotropium L.
1600 H. steudneri Vatke

VERBENACEAE
7138000 Verbena L.
100 V. bonariensis L.
200 V. brasiliensis Vell.
7144000 Lantana L.
600 L. rugosa Thunb.
7145000 Lippia L.
100 L. javanica (Burm. f.)
Spreng.
400 L. rehmannii H. Pearson
7148000 Plexipus Rafin.
600 P. hederaceus (Sond.) R.
Fernandes var. natalensis
(H. Pearson) R. Fernandes
7153000 Priva Adans.

300 P. cordifolia (L. f.) Druce var.
abyssinica (Jaub. & Spach)
Moldenke
7162000 Duranta L.
50 D. erecta L.
7186000 Vitex L.
500 V. mombassae Vatke
800 V. pooara Corbishley
900 V. rehmannii Guerke
7191000 Clerodendrum L.
800 C. glabrum E. Mey. var.
glabrum
1100 C. myricoides (Hochst.) Vatke
1700 C. triphyllum (Harv.) H.
Pearson var. triphyllum

LAMIACEAE
7236000 Acrotome Benth.
300 A. hispida Benth.
7264000 Leonotis (Pers.) R. Br.
1100 L. leonurus (L.) R. Br.
7268000 Leucas Burm. ex R. Br.
700 L. sexdentata Skan
7281000 Stachys L.
2500 S. natalensis Hochst. var.
galpinii (Briq.) Codd
2600 S. natalensis Hochst. var.
natalensis
7290000 Salvia L.
800 S. coccinea Etl.
7339000 Tetradenia Benth.
300 T. brevispicata (N.E. Br.) Codd
7345000 Aeollanthus Mart. ex K.
Spreng.
500 A. parvifolius Benth.
7347000 Pycnostachys Hook.
200 P. reticulata (E. Mey.) Benth.
7350000 Plectranthus L'Hér.
1300 P. fruticosus L'Hér.
1550 P. hadiensis (Forssk.)
Schweinf. ex Spreng. var.
hadiensis
1600 P. hereroensis Engl.
1950 P. madagascariensis (Pers.)
Benth. var. ramosior Benth.
3500 P. tetragonus Gürke
3700 P. verticillatus (L. f.) Druce
7365000 Hemizygia (Benth.) Briq.
400 H. canescens (Guerke) Ashby
2000 H. pretoriae (Guerke) Ashby
subsp. pretoriae
7366000 Ocimum L.
100 O. canum Sims.
7366010 Becium Lindl.
100 B. angustifolium (Benth.)
N.E. Br.
290 B. grandiflorum (Lam.) Pichi-
Serm. var. obovatum (E. Mey.
ex Benth.) Sebald
7367000 Orthosiphon Benth.
300 O. labiatus N.E. Br.

SOLANACEAE
7407000 Solanum L.
2700 S. giganteum Jacq.
3200 S. incanum L.
4900 S. panduriforme E. Mey.
5300 S. retroflexum Dunal
5400 S. rigescens Jacq.
6000 S. sisymbrifolium Lam.

7415000 Datura L.
600 D. stramonium L.

SCROPHULARIACEAE (PART A)
7476000 Nemesia Vent.
2500 N. fruticans (Thunb.) Benth.
7477000 Diclis Benth.
200 D. reptans Benth.
7494000 Teedia Rudolphi
100 T. lucida (Sol.) Rudolphi
7497000 Freylinia Colla
200 F. tropica S. Moore
7519000 Sutera Roth
2500 S. caerulea (L. f.) Hiern
6450 S. levis Hiern
8500 S. palustris Hiern
7522010 Melanospermum Hilliard
100 M. foliosum (Benth.) Hilliard
7523000 Zaluzianskya F.W. Schmidt
1150 Z. elongata Hilliard & Burtt
7560000 Craterostigma Hochst.
200 C. plantagineum Hochst.
7561000 Torenia L.
200 T. spicata Engl.
7597010 Alectra Thunb.
1100 A. orobanchoides Benth.

SELAGINACEAE
7566000 Hebenstretia L.
50 H. angolensis Rolfe
7568000 Selago L.
1400 S. capitellata Schltr.
7568010 Walafrida E. Mey.
3000 W. tenuifolia Rolfe

SCROPHULARIACEAE (PART B)
7616000 Sopubia Buch.-Ham. ex D. Don
100 S. cana Harv. var. cana
400 S. simplex (Hochst.) Hochst.
7622000 Buchnera L.
100 B. ciliolata Engl.
700 B. reducta Hiern
7625000 Striga Lour.
300 S. bilabiata (Thunb.) Kuntze
450 S. elegans Benth.
600 S. gesnerioides (Willd.) Vatke
ex Engl.

BIGNONIACEAE
7722000 Rhigozum Burch.
100 R. brevispinosum Kuntze
200 R. obovatum Burch.
7725000 Jacaranda Juss.
100 J. mimosifolia D. Don.

PEDALIACEAE
7777000 Sesamum L.
200 S. alatum Thonn.
7778000 Ceratotheca Endl.
500 C. triloba (Bernh.) Hook. f.
7780000 Dicerocaryum Boj.
170 D. senecioides (Klotzsch)
Abels subsp. senecioides

GESNERIACEAE
7823000 Streptocarpus Lindl.
2600 S. micranthus C.B. Cl.
4400 S. rimicola Story
4800 S. vanderleurii Bak. f. &
S. Moore

ACANTHACEAE

7914000	Thunbergia Retz.
400	T. atriplicifolia E. Mey. ex Nees
7941000	Chaetacanthus Nees
200	C. costatus Nees
300	C. setiger (Pers.) Lindl.
7965000	Ruellia L.
300	R. cordata Thunb.
800	R. patula Jacq.
7972000	Crabbea Harv.
100	C. acaulis N.E. Br.
200	C. angustifolia Nees
300	C. hirsuta Harv.
7973000	Barleria L.
700	B. bremekampii Oberm.
800	B. crossandriformis C.B. Clarke
1400	B. galpinii C.B. Clarke
3200	B. obtusa Nees
3600	B. pretoriensis C.B. Cl.
4500	B. saxatilis Oberm.
5100	B. transvaalensis Oberm.
7978000	Sclerochiton Harv.
300	S. ilicifolius A. Meeuse
7980000	Blepharis Juss.
2840	B. integrifolia (L. f.) E. Mey. ex Schinz var. integrifolia
3200	B. maderaspatensis (L.) B. Heyne ex Roth subsp. maderaspatensis var. maderaspatensis
3300	B. maderaspatensis (L.) B. Heyne ex Roth subsp. rubiifolia (Schumach.) Napper
4900	B. subvolubilis C.B. Cl. var. longifolia
7985000	Crossandra Salisb.
200	C. greenstockii S. Moore
100	C. fruticulosa Lindau
8026000	Peristrophe Nees.
400	P. transvaalensis (C.B. Clarke) K. Balkwill
8031000	Dicliptera Juss.
300	D. eenii S. Moore
8032000	Hypoestes Soland. ex R. Br.
200	H. forskaolii (Vahl.) R. Br.
8094000	Justicia L.
1400	J. flava (Vahl.) Vahl.
	J. heterocarpa T. Anderson subsp. dinteri (S. Moore) Hedrén
2900	J. protracta (Nees) T. Anderson subsp. protracta

PLANTAGINACEAE

8116000	Plantago L.
400	P. lanceolata L.

RUBIACEAE

8136060	Kohautia Cham. & Schlechtd.
100	K. amatymbica Eckl. & Zeyh.
800	K. cynanchica DC.
1600	K. virgata (Willd.) Brem.
8136140	Agathisanthemum Klotzsch
100	A. bojeri Klotzsch subsp. bojeri
8136200	Oldenlandia L.
750	O. herbacea (L.) Roxb. var. herbacea
1400	O. rupicola (Sond.) Kuntze var. rupicola

8278000	Tarenna Gaertn.
400	T. supra-axillaris (Hemsl.) Bremek. subsp. barbertonensis (Bremek.) Bridson
8285000	Gardenia Ellis
950	G. volkensii K. Schum. subsp. spatulifolia (Stapf & Hutch.) Verdc.
8285010	Rothmannia Thunb.
100	R. capensis Thunb.
8308000	Tricalysia A. Rich.
600	T. junodii (Schinz) Brenan var. junodii
700	T. lanceolata (Sond.) Burtt Davy
8348000	Pentanisia Harv.
100	P. angustifolia (Hochst.) Hochst.
8351000	Vangueria Juss.
400	V. infausta Burch. subsp. infausta
8351020	Pygmaeothamnus Robyns
400	P. zeyheri (Sond.) Robyns var. zeyheri
8351030	Tapiphyllum Robyns
100	T. parvifolium (Sond.) Robyns
8352000	Canthium Lam.
300	C. gilfillanii (N.E. Br.) O.B. Miller
600	C. inerme (L. f.) Kuntze
800	C. mundianum Cham. & Schlechtd.
1300	C. suberosum Codd
8352030	Psydrax Gaertn
200	P. livida (Hiern) Bridson
8359000	Pachystigma Hochst.
800	P. triflorum Robyns
8359010	Fadogia Schweinf.
50	F. homblei De Wild.
8383000	Pavetta L.
1900	P. eylesii S. Moore
2030	P. gardeniifolia A. Rich. var. gardeniifolia
2070	P. gardeniifolia A. Rich. var. subtomentosa K. Schum.
2900	P. lanceolata Eckl.
4300	P. zeyheri Sond.
8435000	Galopina
200	G. circaeoides Thunb.
8438000	Anthospermum L.
1100	A. hispidulum E. Mey. ex Sond.
1800	A. rigidum Eckl. & Zeyh. subsp. rigidum
8464000	Richardia L.
100	R. brasiliensis Gomes
8475000	Spermacoce Gaertn.
300	S. senesis (Klotzsch) Hiern

DIPSACACEAE

8541000	Cephalaria Roem. & Schult.
1300	C. zeyheriana Szabó
8546000	Scabiosa L.
600	S. columbaria L.

CUCURBITACEAE

8564000	Zehneria Endl.
100	Z. marlothii (Cogn.) R. & A. Fern.
8591000	Momordica L.

100	M. balsamina L.
8599000	Cucumis L.
200	C. anguria L. var. anguria
1600	C. zeyheri Sond.
8628000	Coccinia Wight & Arn.
100	C. adoensis (A. Rich.) Cogn.

CAMPANULACEAE

8668000	Wahlenbergia Schrad. ex Roth.
1400	W. buseriana Schltr. & V. Brehm.
6600	W. lycopodioides Schltr. & Brehmer
13100	W. undulata (L. f.) A. DC.

LOBELIACEAE

8694000	Lobelia L.
600	L. aquaemontis E. Wimm.
2800	L. erinus L.
8695000	Monopsis Salisb.
525	M. decipiens (Sond.) Thulin

ASTERACEAE

8751000	Vernonia Schreb.
600	V. anisochaetoides Sond.
1550	V. galpinii Klatt
2000	V. hirsuta (DC.) Sch. Bip. ex Walp.
2400	V. natalensis Sch. Bip. ex Walp.
3000	V. oligocephala (DC.) Sch. Bip. ex Walp.
3075	V. poskeana Vatke & Hildebr. subsp. botswanica Pope
3700	V. staehelinoides Harv.
8795000	Ageratum L.
200	A. houstonianum Mill.
8816010	Stomatanthes R.M. King & H. Robinson
100	S. africanus (Oliv. & Hiern) R.M. King & H. Rob.
8900000	Aster L.
1400	A. harveyanus Kuntze
2000	A. peglerae H. Bol.
8919000	Felicia Cass.
3900	F. fascicularis DC.
6900	F. muricata (Thunb.) Nees subsp. muricata
7000	F. muricata (Thunb.) Nees subsp. strictifolia Grau
8923000	Psiadia Jacq.
100	P. punctulata (DC.) Oliver & Hiern ex Vatke
8925000	Nidorella Cass.
100	N. anomala Steez.
800	N. hottentatica DC.
1500	N. resedifolia DC. subsp. resedifolia
8926000	Conyza Less.
300	C. bonariensis (L.) Cronq.
1625	C. scabrida DC.
8929000	Nolletia Cass.
600	N. rarifolia (Turcz.) Steez
8936000	Brachylaena R. Br.
400	B. huillensis O. Hoffm.
700	B. rotundata S. Moore
8937000	Tarchonanthus
200	T. trilobus DC. var. galpinii (Hutch. & E. Phillips) Paiva
8992050	Pseudognaphalium Kirp.

100	P. luteo-album (L.) Hilliard & Burtt
9006000	Helichrysum Mill.
70	H. acutatum DC.
1870	H. aureonitens Sch. Bip.
2400	H. caespititium (DC.) Harv.
2870	H. cephaloideum DC.
3700	H. coriaceum Harv.
4350	H. dasymallum Hilliard
5100	H. epapposum H. Bol.
7625	H. harveyanum Wild
8500	H. kraussii Sch. Bip.
9700	H. lepidissimum S. Moore
11200	H. mixtum (Kuntze) Moeser var. mixtum
12100	H. nudifolium (L.) Less.
14130	H. pilosellum (L. f.) Less.
16900	H. setosum Harv.
20300	H. uninervium Burtt Davy
21200	H. zeyheri Less.
9037000	Stoebe L.
3300	S. vulgaris Levyns
9055000	Athrixia Ker-Gawl.
500	A. elata Sond.
900	A. phylicoides DC.
9090000	Geigeria Griesellich
700	G. burkei Harv. subsp. burkei var. burkei
1100	G. burkei Harv. subsp. burkei var. zeyheri (Harv.) Merxm.
1500	G. elongata Alston
9094000	Callilepis DC.
600	C. leptophylla Harv.
9148000	Xanthium L.
200	X. strumarium L.
9190000	Blainvillea Cass.
100	B. gayana Cass.
9237000	Bidens L.
100	B. bipinnata L.
500	B. pilosa L.
9291000	Schkuhria Roth
100	S. pinnata (Lam.) Cabr.
9311000	Tagetes L.
200	T. minuta L.
9336000	Phymaspermum Less. Emend. Kallersjo
220	P. bolusii (Hutch.) Källersjö
9356000	Schistostephium Less.
200	S. crataegifolium (DC.) Fenzl. ex Harv.
600	S. heptalobum (DC.) Oliv. & Hiern
9406000	Cineraria L.
1900	C. lobata L'Hérit.
9411000	Senecio L.
1000	S. affinis DC.
2900	S. babertonicus Klatt.
6000	S. consanguineus DC.
5900	S. conrathii N.E. Br.
6300	S. coronatus (Thunb.) Harv.
8000	S. digitalifolius DC.
9100	S. erubescens Aiton var. crepidifolius DC.
11100	S. glanduloso-pilosus Volkens & Muschl.
13100	S. inaequidens DC.
18500	S. othonniflorus DC.
18800	S. oxyriifolius DC.
20600	S. pleistocephalus S. Moore
19800	S. pentactinus Klatt

23650	S. ruwenzoriensis S. Moore
24800	S. sisymbriifolius DC.
27500	S. venosus Harv.
9417000	Euryops Cass.
4700	E. laxus (Harv.) Burtt Davy
6900	E. pedunculatus N.E. Br.
9426000	Garuleum Cass.
1100	G. woodii Schinz
9427000	Osteospermum L.
3500	O. jucundum (E. Phillips) Norl.
5900	O. scariosum DC. var. scariosum
9431000	Ursinia Gaertn.
2400	U. nana DC. subsp. leptophylla Prassler
2500	U. nana DC. subsp. nana
9434000	Gazania Gaertn.
800	G. krebsiana Less. subsp. serrulata (DC.) Rössl.
9435000	Hirpicium Cass.
200	H. bechuanense (S. Moore) Roessler
9438000	Berkheya Ehrh.
1900	B. carlinopsis Welw. ex O. Hoffm. subsp. magalismontana (H. Bol.) Rössl.
4700	B. insignis (Harv.) Thell.
6500	B. radula (Harv.) De Wild.
7500	B. seminivea Harv. & Sond.
9400	B. zeyheri (Sond. & Harv.) Oliv. & Hiern subsp. zeyheri
9501000	Dicoma Cass.
100	D. anomala Sond.
1000	D. galpinii Wilson
2700	D. zeyheri Sond. subsp. zeyheri
9528000	Gerbera L.
100	G. ambigua (Cass.) Sch. Bip.
1250	G. piloselloides (L.) Cass.
1700	G. viridifolia (DC.) Sch. Bip. subsp. viridifolia
9561000	Tolpis Adans.
100	T. capensis (L.) Sch. Bip.

Total: 1004 species

CONFIRMED

Family Mormyridae
Marcusenius macrolepidotus | Bulldog | Snawelvis

Family Cyprinidae | **Barbs, Yellowfishes, Labeos**
Barbus brevipinnis | Shortfin Barb | Kortvin-ghieliemientjie
Barbus bifrenatus | Hyphen Barb | Skakel-ghieliemientjie
Barbus trimaculatus | Threespot Barb | Driekol-ghieliemientjie
Barbus mattozi | Papermouth | Papierbek of silwervis
Barbus marequensis | Largescale Yellowfish | Grootskub-geelvis
Labeo cylindricus | Redeye Labeo | Rooioog-moddervis

Family Clariidae | **Airbreathing Catfishes**
Clarias gariepinus | Sharptooth Catfish | Skerptandbaber (Baber)

Family Cichlidae | **Cichlids**
Chetia flaviventris | Canary Kurper | Kanariekurper
Tilapia sparrmanii | Banded Tilapia | Vleikurper

EXPECTED

Family Anguillidae | **Freshwater Eels**
Anguilla mosambica | Longfin Eel | Geelbek-paling

Family Cyprinidae | **Barbs, Yellowfishes, Labeos**
Barbus paludinosus | Straightfin Barb | Lynvin of Moerasghieliemientjie
Labeo rosae | Rednose Labeo | Rooineus-moddervis
Labeo molybdinus | Leaden Labeo | Loodvis

Family Amphiliidae | **Mountain Catfishes**
Amphilius uranoscopus | Common or Stargazer | Gewone Bergbaber

Family Cyprinodontidae | **Topminnows**
Aplocheilichthys johnstoni | Johnston's Topminnow | Johnston se Lampogie

Family Cichlidae | **Cichlids**
Pseudocrenilabrus philander | Southern Mouthbrooder | Suidelike Mondbroeier

Family Centrarchidae | **Basses and Sunfishes**
Micropterus dolomieu | Smallmouth Bass | Kleinbek-baars

OCCASIONAL

Family Cyprinidae | **Barbs, Yellowfishes, Labeos**
Barbus annectens | Broadstriped Barb | Breëstreep Ghieliemientjie
Barbus unitaeniatus | Longbeard Barb | Langbaard-ghieliemientjie
Barbus afrohamiltoni | Hamilton's Barb | Hamilton se Ghieliemientjie
Barbus polylepis | Smallscale Yellowfish | Kleinskub-geelvis
Labeo ruddi | Silver Labeo | Silwer-moddervis

Family Shilbeidae | **Butter Catfishes**
Schilbe intermedius | Silver Catfish (Butter Barbel) | Silwerbaber (Botterbaber, Makriel)

Family Mochokidae | **Squeakers, Suckermouth Catlets**
Chiloglanis paratus | Neumann's Suckermouth | Zambezi-suierbekkie
Chiloglanis pretoriae | Shortspine Suckermouth | Kortstekel-suierbekkie

Family Cichlidae | **Cichlids**
Tilapia rendalli | Redbreast Tilapia | Rooiborskurper
Oreochromis mossambicus | Mozambique Tilapia | Bloukurper

TO MANAGE

African Parks is an organisation that assists Governments in Africa to manage their National Parks on a long term, well financed and professional basis.

It respects the ownership and responsibilities of the State and the ecological requirements of each National Park.

The projects – like Marakele – are based on a public-private partnership and are managed in accordance with internationally accepted business rules on discipline, budget control, annual reports and transparency.

African Parks commits long term management and know-how to the projects, supported by financial instruments. If a project becomes profitable, this surplus is re-invested into the project.

African Parks works under the following rules for its people:

Keep things simple.

Avoid paperflows.

Bad news must travel fast, good news may travel slowly.

Delegate responsibilities to the workplace.

Do not punish for mistakes, they are the best learning material.

Loyalty, integrity and respect for other cultures are fundamental to all our relationships.

African Parks is a non-political organisation, is open and transparent to third parties, especially to the Government and the media.

WITHOUT PETER, JULIA, HECTOR, CLIVE, WITHOUT NORMAN, LOUIS, GREG AND WENDY, ERWIN, WITHOUT PETER, PIET AND KLAAS, MIKE, MARIUS, MICHELLE, JOHN, DAVID, NICHOLAS, IVAN AND JOHN HENRY, ANTHONY, MURPHY AND HANNES, JOHAN AND JOHANNES, BISHOP, SARAH, BOY, MARKUS, BRENDAN, ELEANOR, AND ANOTHER PETER, CHANTELLE AND BRADLEY, WITHOUT SO MANY OTHERS, BLACK, WHITE, COLOURED, SHORT OR LONG, MALE OR FEMALE, EMPLOYED OR JUST HELPING, THIS PROJECT WOULD NOT HAVE BEEN CONCLUDED, AND WITHOUT THE CHILDREN OF THE LOCAL SCHOOLS, AND MR. SMITS IT WOULD NOT HAVE BEEN SUCH FUN.

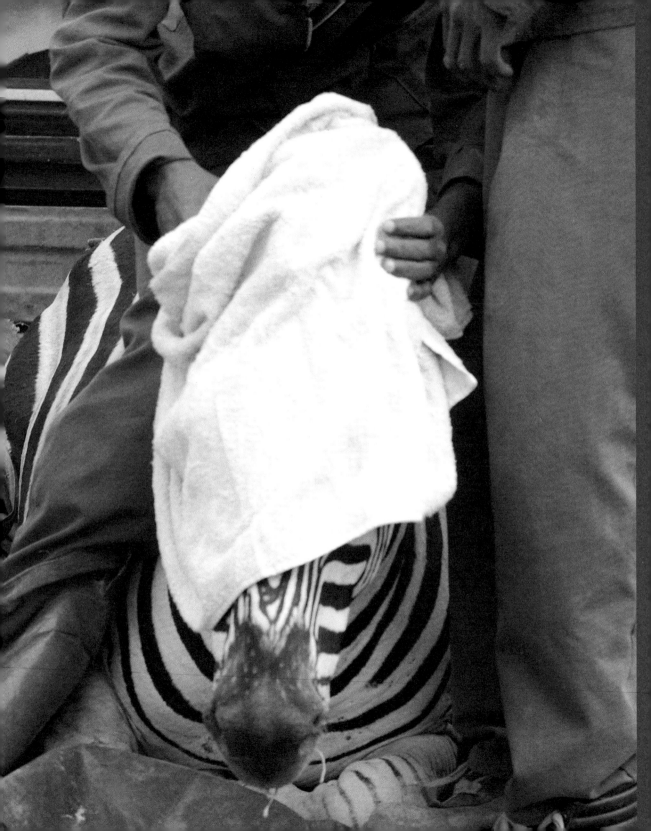

FOR GENERAL INFORMATION ABOUT
AFRICAN PARKS PLEASE CONTACT:
info@africanparks-conservation.com

FOR INFORMATION ABOUT VISITING MARAKELE
YOU CAN CONSULT OUR WEBSITE AT:
www.marakelepark.co.za